WHEN YOU READ THIS BOOK

The Jewish Torah Is Not the Word of God

I. D. CAMPBELL

ISBN-13: 978-1490459424
ISBN-10: 1490459421

TABLE OF CONTENTS

BISMILLAHI RAHMANI RAHEEM-IN THE NAME OF ALLAH MOST GRACIOUS, MOST MERCIFUL

This book is dedicated to Yahya Luqman Saleem

IF YOU OPEN YOUR HEART AND YOU OPEN YOUR MIND, WHEN YOU READ THIS BOOK IT WILL OPEN YOUR EYES

ACKNOWLEDGMENTS

First and foremost, ALHAMDULILLAH. ALL PRAISE IS DUE TO ALLAH. He is the source of all truth, therefore all that I convey of the truth in this book and in life are because of ALLAH, and only the mistakes are from me.

MY INTENTIONS

Al-Quran 2:79 Then woe to those who write the Book with their own hands, and then say: "This is from Allah"

The first item of discussion is the Jewish Torah's claim to be from God. It describes the dialogue between God and man on several occasions, but does it say all these words are from God or inspired by God? The answer is a resounding, no. Why then are these words considered to be the words of God and is the author of these writings qualified to be God's mouthpiece for mankind? As to why these words are understood by many to be the unequivocal words of God, this question is a rhetoric one, just for pondering purposes. Yet the enquiry about the writer of the Jewish Torah is a question that needs to be answered. The authorship has been commonly attributed to Moses (pbuh). Though his traditional character seems to give him qualification as a man in whom God may entrust His message to be delivered, scholars of the Bible reject this view. It will be one goal in this book to demonstrate that in fact, Moses (pbuh) did not write the books attributed to him. If we trust in the expertise of the scholars, then we can conclude that the Bible may qualify in the description of the scriptures mention in the Quranic verse above.

But the proof that Moses (pbuh) did not write the Jewish Torah doesn't necessarily discount the idea that God is the author of these five books. The anonymity of the author harms the credibility of the Jewish Torah, but it does not completely negate the possibility that God authored or inspired this book to an unknown individual. It is my intention to demonstrate that it is quite improbable that God authored or inspired these books of the Bible. Although I believe the remaining books of the Bible contain a multitude of elements contrary to the dignity and prestige one might expect from a book of God, I find it more manageable to concentrate on the first five books of the Bible.

Hopefully this book will encourage the reader to examine other books of the Bible and determine for themselves if they are worthy of God's signature and/or approval. Because of the importance bestowed upon the Jewish Torah and its traditional author and main character, Moses (pbuh), by Jews, this book is obviously more provocative to them. But I hope that the co-owner of these scriptures, the Christians, take note of this book as well, as Jesus (pbuh) said quoting Deuteronomy 8:3 in

Matthew 4:4 But he answered and said, It is written, Man shall not live by bread alone, but by every word that proceedeth out of the mouth of God.

It is the prerogative of some Christians to discount what they call the Old Testament or the old covenant as out of date thus it is replaced by the New Testament or new covenant. Though Jesus (pbuh) revised a few laws of the Jewish Torah, he endorsed the laws as a whole, and commanded their adherence down to the smallest detail. He went so far as to declare blessing upon those who teach and obey the laws and condemnation upon those who disobey the laws and teach other to do the same. In fact, his revision in some instances were made more strict than the original law in order for his disciples, who were all Jews, to surpass the piety of other Jews of his time (Matt. 5:17-6:17).

Nonetheless, my intentions are to present the truth as I see it with complete honesty and integrity. What is of equal importance is to admit that though I feel great conviction in the stance in which I am taking in this book, this is my opinion and my perspective on the matter at hand. Thus it is completely open to debate. In fact, I expect such. Contemplation, reason and discussion are the ways in which we arrive at the truth.

Isaiah 1:18 Come now, and let us reason together

It should be pointed out that I am a Muslim and I believe the Glorious Qur'an to be the words of God. In light of the fact that I embark upon the challenge of distinguishing God's inspiration from the Jewish Torah, I am not naïve enough to consider the probability of such a challenge waged against the book in which I place my faith. And in the pursuit of truth and following the tradition of the Glorious Qur'an, I invite this challenge.

Al-Quran 4:82 Do they not consider the Qur'an (with care)? Had it been from other Than Allah, they would surely have found therein Much discrepancy.

The Qur'an asks those who doubt it to find any discrepancies in it. But this kind of challenge will not be a refutation of the book in which I am writing. In other words, if one is able to produce a discrepancy, an untruth, or contradiction in the Quran, this in no way gives justification for possible errors in the Jewish Torah. It only means that both books contain errors and should not be considered to be the words of God. I am writing this book as if my audience consists of people from every spectrum of belief or disbelief. Therefore I make my case so an atheist or agnostic would understand it. And in their eyes, possible errors in the Quran have absolutely no merit in the discussion of the validity of the Jewish Torah. I have partaking in numerous debates and this seems to be an issue many times. And I am still a Muslim, not despite the commonality of errors between the Bible and the Quran but through discussion, I found that the Quran did not contain the errors many so adamantly proclaimed that it had. I too am adamant in my proclamations. Yet conviction is not a precise tool for measuring the truth. We must demand explanations and proof and more explanation and even more proof. The topic in discussion is not to be taking lightly. Religion is something people hold as dear and sacred. With this in mind, I place the burden upon myself to concisely present my proof and the explanations of them and to show how the understanding of the Jewish Torah affects the world today.

I.D. Campbell
June 2009

INTRODUCTION TO THE JEWISH TORAH

The Hebrew Scriptures are called the "Tanakh" which is actually an acronym made up by the first Hebrew alphabet from Jewish Torah (The Teachings), Nevi'im (The Prophets), and Kethuvim (the writings). These scriptures contain the same books as the Christian's Old Testament (this name is not endorsed by Jews), but they are arranged in a different order in the Tanakh. Here is the order in which they appear.

The Jewish Torah
1. Genesis
2. Exodus
3. Leviticus
4. Numbers
5. Deuteronomy

Nevi'im
6. Joshua
7. Judges
8. Samuel
9. Kings
10. Isaiah
11. Jeremiah
12. Ezekiel
13. The Twelve Minor Prophets
    - Hosea
    - Joel
    - Amos
    - Obadiah
    - Jonah
    - Micah
    - Nahum
    - Habakkuk
    - Zephaniah

Haggai
Zechariah
Malachi

Kesuvim

14. Psalms
15. Proverbs
16. Job
17. Song of Songs
18. Ruth
19. Lamentations
20. Ecclesiastes
21. Esther
22. Daniel
23. Ezra (includes Nehemiah)
24. Chronicles

The Jewish Torah, meaning teaching or doctrine, is also called the "Humas" or "Chumash" coming from the Hebrew word "chamesh" meaning five. Another name commonly used for the JewishTorah is the Pentateuch, which is Greek for "five volumes." Throughout this book, when I mention the Jewish Torah, it is indicative of the first five books of the Bible, unless it is stated otherwise. I will begin with the book of Genesis.

GENESIS

CREATION

This scripture begins with a description of the creation of the universe, its contents and its inhabitants. In the light of science, it is extremely difficult to believe that God created the universe and its components in the sequence presented in the book of Genesis. The first obstacle to hurdle is that the events are said to take place in 24 hour intervals. The words "on the first day" signify that in the first twenty four hours God created the heavens and the earth and gave them light. Genesis maintains that creation was completed in six days. This means the entire universe and everything in it was created in 144 hours. Considering that scientists insist that this process took millions upon millions of years to form, some Bible scholars conclude that the word "day" used in the description of creation is used as an indication of a long period of time. And the Hebrew word for day, *yom*, does have such a connotation. However the context in which the word is used shows that the author intended to convey the message of a day as in 24 hours. This is evident when we read:

1:4 And G-d saw the light that it was good; and G-d divided the light from the darkness.
1:5 And G-d called the light Day, and the darkness He called Night And there was evening and there was morning, one day.

On the first day of creation, Genesis says there was night and morning, which would indicate that this is a 24 hour day because the earth must be already on its axis and in rotation around the sun in order for there to be morning and evening. And thereafter, God continues creating different aspects of the earth and universe every day with each phase called the second day, the third day, etc. This is ended after the sixth day. On the seventh day, God is said to have rested, which is also objectionable in my view.

2:3 And G-d blessed the seventh day, and hallowed it; because that in it He rested from all His work which G-d in creating had made.

This day is commemorated as the Sabbath of the Jews in which they do not work each Saturday of the week, as God did not work of this day. This is another proof that the words of the creation are taken literally here by Jews. As for the sequence of creation, God amazingly creates light before he creates the sun and stars (1:3-4, 13-18). This is placing the creation of light before the creation of its light bulb. Equally intriguing is the creation of vegetation and trees on day three, which is before creating their source of life, the sun (1:11-12). The sun and the moon are finally made on day four. One could reply that God can do anything. But why would he do such a thing? When he made the first humans, he did not create them as helpless babies.

It is improbable that the egg was made before the chicken. How would the egg hatch and how would it survive? In like manner, how would vegetation and trees survive without the sun for two periods spanning millions of years? It is apparent that the author is assuming that this period is 48 hours in which case the creation remains illogically sequenced but much easier to grasp. Another thing to ponder is that on the fourth day, it is said that God created two great lights. What scientists now know is that the moon does not produce light at all. In fact, it is a reflector of the light from the sun. Therefore it is more accurate to say God created 1 light and 1 reflector of light. This may simply be a matter of interpretation but it is no small matter to state that day and night were formed before the sun and moon (1:5, 1:16).

We also find on the sixth day that God created man in God's image (1:26). The phrase "in our image" in this verse means man is formed and born to be just and righteous as God is just and righteous. Also the plural used in this phrase is the "royal we" which does not denote any deviation of the oneness of God. It is a plural used in the Hebrew language to show reverence and respect to the subject in discussion. So I find no real difficulty with this verse unless one considers that the invisible God actually has an image.

We read that Adam begot a son "in his own likeness, after his image" (5:3). This expression seems to describe character not outward appearances. The problem arises when I read in the next chapter another narration of the creation of man (2:7).

MORE THAN ONE AUTHOR?

Though the creation is said to have ceased at the beginning of chapter two, the creation of man is revisited later in this chapter. Initially, the second story seems to be an expansion of the first. However, with close analysis, we find a slightly different depiction of creation in chapter two. In this chapter, man is created before animals, which is the exact opposite sequence in the first creation story (2:7-19, 1:19-27). And these animals are made by God to be man's helpers or companions. However this is insufficient for man, so God creates a woman for man. So we have in the first story animals, then the man and woman together. In the second story, God creates man, then animals and then woman.

If we venture into other stories of the scriptures, we find that several of them are told twice, one after the other with varying details. This discovery has prompted many Biblical scholars to conclude that these stories are from different sources and interwoven together in the Tanakh. One observation used to come to this conclusion is the fact that the stories detailing the same event contain different names for God. For example, Noah (pbuh) is commanded by "Elohim" to put two pairs of every animal on the ark (6:19-22). But "Hashem" commanded Noah (pbuh) to place seven pairs of every animal on earth, aside from the unclean animals, in which he was to take two pairs (7:1-2). Hashem literally means "the name" in Hebrew. It is used as a substitute for the tetragammaton, "YHWH" which is forbidden to be pronounced in the Jewish religion. Many times it is replaced with the word "Lord." In any case, Elohim tells Noah (pbuh) one thing and Hashem tells him another. There are other instances of suspicious redundancy as well, such as Noah (pbuh), his family and the animals are loaded on the ark twice (6:18-22 , 7:7), God states that the world is corrupt twice (6:5-7, 6:11-13), the Ten Commandments are repeated twice (Ex. 20:2-17, Deut. 5:6-21), the Abraham (pbuh), Sarah and the King story (Gen. 12:11-20, 20:2-12), God's covenant with Abraham (pbuh) is repeated twice (15:18, 17:7), and the naming of Beersheba is done twice (Gen. 21:25-31, 26:19-33). Many scholars maintain that there exist not only doublets, but triplets in the five books of the Jewish Torah. This suggests at least three different authors, but that's not all. In reading the book of Deuteronomy, we witness a work totally different in its style from the other four books, thus giving rise to the hypothesis of a fourth author. These different authors are characterized by their style and emphasis on different aspects of their narrative. It is believed that the different stories and laws were transmitted orally with a certain prejudice by their author to emphasize and minimize the aspects they saw fit and these traditions are combined into what we have today. Bible scholars separate them in the following manner.

J-The Jahwist J describes a human-like God called Yahweh and has a special interest in Judah and in the Aaronid priesthood. J has an extremely eloquent style. J uses an earlier form of the Hebrew language than P.

E-The Elohist E describes a human-like God initially called El (which sometimes appears as Elohim according to the rules of Hebrew grammar), and called Yahweh subsequent to the incident of the burning bush. E focuses on biblical Israel and on the Shiloh priesthood. E has a moderately eloquent style. E uses an earlier form of the Hebrew language than P.

P-The Priestly source P describes a distant and unmerciful God, sometimes referred to as Elohim or as El Shaddai. P partly duplicates J and E, but alters details to suit P's opinion, and also consists of most of Leviticus. P has its main interest in an Aaronid priesthood and in King

Hezekiah. P has a low level of literary style, and has an interest in lists and dates.

D-The Deuteronomist D consists of most of Deuteronomy. D probably also wrote the Deuteronomistic history (Josh, Judg, 1 & 2 Sam, 1 & 2 Kgs). D has a particular interest in the Shiloh priesthood and in King Josiah. D uses a form of Hebrew similar to that of P, but in a different literary style.

Bible scholar and author, Richard E. Friedman, in his book, "Who Wrote the Bible" has written extensively on the subject at hand. As with every proposition, there is opposition. It must be stated that there are several Bible scholars who write this idea off as total speculation, and invariably conclude that the Jewish Torah had one author. And each side continues to produce evidence to support their case. But my point in mentioning this "Modern Documentary Hypothesis" is to show that there is a dispute raging amongst Biblical scholars as to which human being wrote the Jewish Torah, so it should be no surprise as to why I question whether or not God wrote or inspired it. I myself am not a Biblical scholar, but I would like to throw my two cents into the conversation. Though I find the multiple authors argument more plausible, I have greater interest in whether or not Moses (pbuh) wrote these books. And even the Bible scholars who postulate that there is but one author, they find it difficult to conclude that Moses (pbuh) was that author. Moses' (pbuh) character is introduced in Exodus. In discussing that book, I will begin to examine the possibility that Moses (pbuh) is the author of these works.

ADAM (pbuh), EVE AND THE TREES

Now in Genesis 2:9, we are told of the "tree of knowledge of good and evil" and the "tree of life" in the midst of an abundance of trees in the Garden of Eden. Let us explore the tree of knowledge of good and evil, first. God tells the first man, Adam, that he may eat from any tree in the garden except the tree of knowledge and if he eats from this tree, he will die. Human's natural instinct is to ask, "Why?" When reading this story I was wondering, why could Adam not eat from the tree? Was it because the fruit would kill him or was death merely a consequence and not the actual reason that this tree is forbidden? Yet Adam (pbuh) doesn't ask for clarification on this matter. Then Eve, his companion, is introduced to the story. And she is tempted by a serpent to eat fruit from the forbidden tree. Though Eve was not present at the time God forbid the fruit to be eaten, she tells the serpent that God says that death is the result of eating or even touching this fruit. Then the serpent insinuates something quite strange. He says in essence that God was lying. He says that Adam (pbuh) and Eve would not die from eating the fruit, but that they will become like God, knowing good and evil. Was this true? Is it possible that the serpent, which is universally considered to be the devil, is telling the truth and exposing a lie pronounced by God? Believing the serpent to be speaking the truth, Eve has eaten the forbidden fruit and she gave some to Adam (pbuh) and he has eaten some of the fruit, as well.

3:8 And they heard the voice of HaShem G-d walking in the garden toward the cool of the day; and the man and his wife hid themselves from the presence of HaShem G-d amongst the trees of the garden.
3:9 And HaShem G-d called unto the man, and said unto him: 'Where art thou?'

At this juncture, Adam (pbuh) and Eve come out from hiding and partially confess to their sins. I say partially because neither of them takes the blame for their actions. Adam (pbuh) blames Eve and Eve blames the serpent. Then God administers punishment for their disobedience.

There are several problems with this story. One of them being that the serpent actually told them the truth. The eating of the fruit gave them knowledge of good and evil. Because immediately after eating, they realized that they were naked, so they sewed fig leaves together and used them as clothes. Before this point "they were both naked, the man and his wife, and were not ashamed". (2:25). That the serpent is truthful is a fact also reiterated by God himself.

3:22 And HaShem G-d said: 'Behold, the man is become as one of us, to know good and evil

When we reevaluate the story, there exist an obvious contradiction to the idea that Adam (pbuh) and Eve did not know the difference between good and evil until after eating this fruit. Obedience to God is obviously good and disobedience is evil and before they ate the fruit, they knew this fact. This is why Eve said "The serpent beguiled me" (3:13). Remember Eve resisted the serpent's request and she recanted the threat God gave Adam (pbuh). With this stated, I would conclude that this is not the words of God, but the words and thoughts of man to explain man's initial understanding of right and wrong. Why would God not want man to be able to distinguish good from evil, in the first place? The serpent and God give the answer, because "ye shall be as G-d" (3:5, 3:22). This presents a paranoid God, which cannot be accepted by any rational believer in the Almighty Creator. Man's knowledge in no way harms the majesty of God. In fact man's knowledge is what brings him closer to the realization of God, especially his knowledge of right and wrong.

The serpent also said that the eating of the fruit would not cause them to die. If we are to assume that God meant that Adam (pbuh) would spiritually, but temporarily die after eating the fruit then there is no problem. I say this because after the sin, God punished him, yet he continued to receive blessings from God (4:1). If God meant that eating from the tree would physically kill him, then there is a problem because Adam (pbuh) lived for hundreds of years after this incident (5:5). Not to mention the fact that Adam (pbuh) was given permission to eat from "every" tree, including the tree of life, which would give him everlasting life. But God has a change of heart and he decides that Adam (pbuh) cannot eat from the tree of life now.

3:22 And HaShem G-d said: 'Behold, the man is become as one of us, to know good and evil; and now, lest he put forth his hand, and take also of the tree of life, and eat, and live for ever.'
3:23 Therefore HaShem G-d sent him forth from the garden of Eden, to till the ground from whence he was taken.
3:24 So He drove out the man; and He placed at the east of the Garden of Eden the cherubim, and the flaming sword which turned every way, to keep the way to the tree of life.

Here again we are given some disparaging images of God. We find that the reason that Adam (pbuh) and Eve are cast from the garden is because God fears that they may eat from the "tree of life" and gain some new attributes as they did from the "tree of knowledge." Thus their expulsion is not due to their crime, but it is a precautionary measure to prevent man from being like God. And God goes so far as to place an angel and a "flaming sword" to guard this tree. This is apparently not the words of God, but of a human being's superstitions and reasoning as to where our morals originate and why all men die? In order to explain the pains of child birth, the reason man must work for food, and why the husband must rule over his wife, the author attributes all these things to the punishment administered by God to the whole of mankind for the sins of two people done thousands of years ago (3:16-19). We do God a great disservice to think of him in such a manner. Even more disturbing is the fact that God seems to be unable to find Adam (pbuh) and Eve, when they "hid" from him. Genesis clearly states that Adam (pbuh) and Eve hid themselves from God. And to further illustrate this point, we read that God asks them, "Where are you?"

Another human error might be Adam's (pbuh) punishment. He is said to be cursed to sweat for his food. However it is stated earlier that work was the reason in which man was made (2:5-15). And to whom is God speaking when he says "Behold, the man is become as one of us?" If God is speaking, who is in this group that he is included in? This is the kind of verse which gives rise to Trinitarian or henotheist implications. Judaism is held as strictly monotheistic and the plurals used by and for God are plurals of respect and reverence, not in the number of Gods. But does the text of the Jewish Torah agree with this explanation? This is another topic we will explore.

GENEALOGIES-LIST OF JEWISH NAMES

Now we read that Adam had two sons, Cain and Abel (4:1-2). Cain became jealous of Abel and he killed his brother. This has been considered to be the first act of murder committed on earth. But this may not be the case, simply because the Jewish Torah does not actually detail the full story of mankind. This is noticed when God places a mark on Cain's head to warn people in other lands not to harm him (4:15). If Adam (pbuh), Eve and Cain are the only people on earth, then it would be unnecessary for Cain to fear any person in another land and unnecessary to have an indicator put on Cain's forehead for Adam (pbuh) and Eve. Adam (pbuh) and Eve had another son named Seth. Seth had a son named Enosh, but where did Seth's wife come from? It seems the author is only interested in recording history from the Hebrew standpoint and through the lineage of those who are to be known as the 12 tribes of Israel. Whole chapters are dedicated to lineage.

5:1 This is the book of the generations of Adam. In the day that G-d created man, in the likeness of G-d made He him;
5:2 male and female created He them, and blessed them, and called their name Adam, in the day when they were created.
5:3 And Adam lived a hundred and thirty years, and begot a son in his own likeness, after his image; and called his name Seth.
5:4 And the days of Adam after he begot Seth were eight hundred years; and he begot sons and daughters.

5:5 And all the days that Adam lived were nine hundred and
thirty years; and he died.
5:6 And Seth lived a hundred and five years, and begot Enosh.
5:7 And Seth lived after he begot Enosh eight hundred and seven
years, and begot sons and daughters.
5:8 And all the days of Seth were nine hundred and twelve years;
and he died.
5:9 And Enosh lived ninety years, and begot Kenan.
5:10 And Enosh lived after he begot Kenan eight hundred and
fifteen years, and begot sons and daughters.
5:11 And all the days of Enosh were nine hundred and five years;
and he died.
5:12 And Kenan lived seventy years, and begot Mahalalel.
5:13 And Kenan lived after he begot Mahalalel eight hundred
and forty years, and begot sons and daughters.
5:14 And all the days of Kenan were nine hundred and ten years;
and he died.
5:15 And Mahalalel lived sixty and five years, and begot Jared.
5:16 And Mahalalel lived after he begot Jared eight hundred and
thirty years, and begot sons and daughters.
5:17 And all the days of Mahalalel were eight hundred ninety and
five years; and he died.
5:18 And Jared lived a hundred sixty and two years, and begot
Enoch.

5:19 And Jared lived after he begot Enoch eight hundred years, and begot sons and daughters.
5:20 And all the days of Jared were nine hundred sixty and two years; and he died.
5:21 And Enoch lived sixty and five years, and begot Methuselah.
5:22 And Enoch walked with G-d after he begot Methuselah three hundred years, and begot sons and daughters.
5:23 And all the days of Enoch were three hundred sixty and five years.
5:24 And Enoch walked with G-d, and he was not; for G-d took him.
5:25 And Methuselah lived a hundred eighty and seven years, and begot Lamech.
5:26 And Methuselah lived after he begot Lamech seven hundred eighty and two years, and begot sons and daughters.
5:27 And all the days of Methuselah were nine hundred sixty and nine years; and he died.
5:28 And Lamech lived a hundred eighty and two years, and begot a son.
5:29 And he called his name Noah, saying: 'This same shall comfort us in our work and in the toil of our hands, which cometh from the ground which HaShem hath cursed.'
5:30 And Lamech lived after he begot Noah five hundred ninety and five years, and begot sons and daughters.

5:31 And all the days of Lamech were seven hundred seventy and seven years; and he died.
5:32 And Noah was five hundred years old; and Noah begot Shem, Ham, and Japheth.

This is just the beginning (4:17-26, 10:6-31, 11:10-27 etc.). Is this a book of God? I am inclined to believe that such things are trivial to God, but significant to man. In a book of God, I expect guidance, inspiration and knowledge. All these things would work cohesively to help mankind reach the ultimate goal of Paradise with God. Merely listing names upon names of people who have no significance to mankind at large seems to be signs of a humanly inspired book. But it does provide a good indication of the Hebrews scriptures stances on when creation began. Through the recorded lineage, the Tanakh suggests that the beginning of creation was roughly 6000 years ago. Unfortunately for science or for the Hebrew Scriptures, scientists insist that this figure is off by about 13 billion years.

NOAH (pbuh)

In chapter 6, we are informed of the "Sons of God" who have traditionally been known as angels who cohabited with earthly women because of their striking beauty. And they begot nephilim, or giants. The words used in this chapter seem to indicate that these fathers and mothers were not of the same nature, thus making extraordinary offspring. The nephilim were nonetheless mortal and at this time, God decrees from this point on that man would only live to the age of "one hundred and twenty years" (6:3), although the Bible records several biblical figures defying this decree (11:11-32). Perhaps God made such a decree because of the wickedness of mankind and the effect it had on him.

6:6 And it repented HaShem that He had made man on the earth, and it grieved Him at His heart.

In this I find a kink in God's armor. This would mean that God made a mistake in making man. Can God make a mistake? Did he not know that man would sin and to what extent he would sin? Yet we read that God regrets making man. And this is a recurring theme in the Hebrew Scriptures, despite the proclamation that God doesn't regret or repent.

Numbers 23:19 G-d is not a man, that He should lie; neither the son of man, that He should repent

As a solution to the strife in God's heart, he decided to wipe the whole of mankind out, save Noah (pbuh), Noah's (pbuh) family and some animals of every species. We have already discussed the discrepancies between the two accounts of Noah (pbuh) and crew on the ship, but what we have not discussed is the magnitude of the flood in which God chose to blot out mankind from "the face of the earth" (6:7). Modern scientists assert that a global flood would contain remnants of its effects all over the world. Proof of the flood is difficult to be shown to exist on a regional level and the accusation that its occurrence spanned the globe multiply this task. This dilemma has forced many to conclude that the flood was regional and not global. The problem is that Genesis insists that the flood engulfed the entire earth (6:17). One could interpret that this mentioning of wiping out everyone on earth was a reference to the Hebrew people because as we have noted the Hebrew people seem to be the only characters in which God holds interest in the Jewish Torah. Whatever the case may be, we are left with Noah (pbuh) and his family.

Noah (pbuh) makes a burnt offering for God and the anthropomorphic nature often attributed to God in the Jewish Torah take shape again. God smells this sweet savor (8:21) and vows to himself to never inflict such a harsh punishment upon the earth and every living thing for man's sake ever again (8:21). This is another example of God's missteps in decision-making. He regrets making man so he kills them, then he regrets killing them. This cannot be words and thoughts inspired by God, for they belittle God's omniscience. Also God's reason for the flood was that every thought of man's imagination was continually evil (6:5). Yet this is also the reason that God decides never to punishment them in such a manner ever again. God is said to have realized later that "the imagination of man's heart is evil from his youth" (8:21). According to the Jewish Torah, God acted out of anger and without full consideration of the problem of man and without full consideration of the consequences of his reaction to this problem.

Noah (pbuh) is a righteous man and is described as one who "walked with God" (6:9, 7:1). He is such an upstanding man of God that God chose him and his family to continue humanity's existence. God builds a covenant with Noah (pbuh). Yet after such a tremendous experience as the flood and this great honor from God, Noah (pbuh) is said to do some quite ungodly and irrational things. Noah (pbuh) promptly builds a vineyard. He gets drunk one night and is frolicking around naked. His son, Ham sees his father and summons his other two brothers, Shem and Japheth. His two brothers cover the father, while making certain not to look at their naked father.

Now in the account I mentioned above of the story, is there any mention of a character by the name of Canaan? Not at all. So it is unreasonable for Noah (pbuh), a righteous man of God, to curse a person not involved in the event at hand, especially in an inebriated mind state. Yet this is what Noah (pbuh) does. He cursed Canaan for no good reason (9:24-25). Now when we read the full story of Noah (pbuh), we do find the name, Canaan, twice before the curse.

9:18 And the sons of Noah, that went forth from the ark, were Shem, and Ham, and Japheth: and Ham is the father of Canaan.
9:22 And Ham, the father of Canaan, saw the nakedness of his father, and told his two brethren without.

It is quite clear that the author is inserting Canaan, Ham's son, into the story with some ulterior motive because there is no mention of Shem and

Japheth's children. The author wishes to have the reader to think of the father and son synonymously, thus a punishment to Ham is a punishment to Canaan. But what was the crime? Many scholar have speculated that Ham saw Noah's (pbuh) wife naked, not Noah's (pbuh) nakedness (Lev. 18:8), but this does not negate the fact that he did nothing wrong, except havehis brothers resolve the situation instead of doing so himself. And Noah (pbuh) was in no position to curse anybody. Had he not been naked and drunk, there would be no matter to resolve. What is astounding is that this man of God curses his own innocent grandson, Canaan, instead of the alleged culprit, Ham. Noah (pbuh) cursed Canaan to be a slave to his brethren (9:25). What cruelty! How was Canaan singled out of Ham's children, seeing that Ham had three other sons (10:6)? Why Canaan the youngest son, instead of the firstborn, Cush? And how could God uphold such an unjust punishment? This particular curse was used by Christian slave masters to justify to the slaves and to themselves the tenants of slavery in America and abroad. The children of Canaan, the Canaanites, are said to be the blacks of Africa, which Noah (pbuh) cursed to be slaves, thus making it permissible under God. There is more to this curse that meets the eye. In a list of the children of Shem, Japheth and Ham, we read about the land and the borders of the Canaanite people (10:19). Remember the Canaanites. This name is reoccurring in the Jewish Torah, denoting its importance.

TOWER OF BABEL

In the book of Genesis, we are told that there was one language for the people of the whole earth. And the people put their minds together and decided to build a city and a tower that would reach to the heavens. Interestingly enough, they also decided to give themselves a name, just in case they are scattered around the earth (11:4). The interesting part is that God "comes down to earth to see the city and the tower" and he does just what they are preparing for. He made them scatter around the earth. But one gets the idea that God is not all-knowing and all-seeing, because he must come to earth to witness this feat. This is the only reason given as to why God came to earth. God coming down to see this tower is as mind-jarring as Cain going "out from the presence of God" (4:16). However on God's visit, he becomes worried about humans making such a tower and working in such unity. The paranoia of God is established again as he says, I assume to himself, the following:

11:6 And HaShem said: 'Behold, they are one people, and they have all one language; and this is what they begin to do; and now nothing will be withholden from them, which they purpose to do.
11:7 Come, let us go down, and there confound their language, that they may not understand one another's speech.'
11:8 So HaShem scattered them abroad from thence upon the face of all the earth; and they left off to build the city.

God is again afraid of the power of man. This author assumed that over the clouds was actually heaven and it was possible to reach it by building a tall tower. Perhaps he thought that if man could gain access to heaven, the "tree of life" was in his grasp. So in order to explain the different languages of man and to explain man's presence around the world, he invents an elaborate story that belittles the majesty of God. This explanation of man's variation in language and his nomadic behavior cannot be taken as truth from God, unless we are to concede that God is in awe and in fear of man's abilities.

After the scattering of man, Genesis immediately refocuses on its main characters. We are given another genealogy which leads us to the patriarch, Abraham (pbuh).

ABRAHAM (pbuh)

12:6 And Abram passed through the land unto the place of Shechem, unto the terebinth of Moreh. And the Canaanite was then in the land.
12:7 And HaShem appeared unto Abram, and said: 'Unto thy seed will I give this land'

God appears to Abram (pbuh), whose names is later changed to Abraham (pbuh), and directs him to the land of CANAAN, and God tells Abram (pbuh), he promises to deliver it to his offspring, despite the fact that the Canaanites were already living there. These are the same Canaanites which are cursed by Noah (pbuh) to be slaves. God not only upholds the curse, but promises Abraham (pbuh) the land in which they live. Though this promise will take years to fulfill, God seems to forgive any sin and take any measure to make sure this land is taken from the Canaanites. It is believed that the Canaanites were a sexually immoral people, thus God makes them disposable. Of course, the idea that they were sexual deviants is declared in the Hebrew Scriptures, which is similar to understanding the American Revolution from the sole standpoint of Americans. The British have a very different understanding of this event in history and the truth is probably somewhere in the middle. However the Jewish Torah does give more details about these hostilities between the early Hebrews and the Canaanites and it gives the description of the land that is to be given to Abraham (pbuh).

10:19 And the border of the Canaanite was from Zidon, as thou goest toward Gerar, unto Gaza; as thou goest toward Sodom and Gomorrah and Admah and Zeboiim, unto Lasha.

Canaan was the name of the region today known as Israel, the West Bank, Gaza, and parts of Lebanon and Syria. This is the land promises to Abraham (pbuh). This promise becomes the underlined theme of the entire Jewish Torah. The author's every story leads to this ultimate goal. A point to be stressed is that the Jewish Torah says God made two slightly different promises, but the significance of that difference is not slight at all. God first promises the land to Abraham's (pbuh) seed (12:7), but later he expands the promise to Abraham (pbuh) and his seed (13:15, 17). Amazingly, this promise is restricted again to his seed (15:18), but expanded a few chapters later (17:8). The problem is that Abraham (pbuh) never received the Promised Land. He died long before the promised was fulfilled, thus the two prophecies which assert that Abraham would get the land were false prophecies. One may attempt to reconcile the verses by stating that giving the land to Abraham's (pbuh) seed is synonymous with Abraham (pbuh) getting the land. However in chapter 17, it states that Abraham (pbuh) and his seed will receive the land, if they were to keep his covenant. God's covenant was to have every male circumcised. If it is understood that giving the promised land to Abraham (pbuh) and his seed is to mean Abraham (pbuh) receives the land, not physically, but through his seed, then the circumcision of his seed, and not himself, should suffice to fulfill the covenant. Of course this is not the case.

17:23 And Abraham took Ishmael his son, and all that were born in his house, and all that were bought with his money, every male among the men of Abraham's house, and circumcised the flesh of their foreskin in the selfsame day, as G-d had said unto him.
17:24 And Abraham was ninety years old and nine, when he was circumcised in the flesh of his foreskin.
17:25 And Ishmael his son was thirteen years old, when he was circumcised in the flesh of his foreskin.
17:26 In the selfsame day was Abraham circumcised, and Ishmael his son.
17:27 And all the men of his house, those born in the house, and those bought with money of a foreigner, were circumcised with him.

Abraham (pbuh) and his seed must keep the covenant, so Abraham (pbuh) and his seed can get the land in this chapter. Also the existence of conflicting prophesies help substantiate the claim that there was more than one author of the book of Genesis. If we are to take a closer look at the end of chapter 17 replicated above, a noticeable redundancy is present as if there were two stories converged. Nonetheless, both prophecies say that the land is promised to Abraham's (pbuh) offspring, but which child?

Abraham (pbuh) was married to a very beautiful woman named Sarah. She was so beautiful that Abraham (pbuh) feared that kings of the land might kill him in order to take her from him. With this fear in mind, Abraham (pbuh) on two occasions told two different kings that Sarah was his sister and not his wife. On both occasions, the kings wanted her, yet God placed a curse on them and their entire household simply because they sought to have Abraham's (pbuh) "sister" (12:11-20, 20:2-12). Had Abraham (pbuh) told the truth, then God would not have cursed them and their household. But shouldn't God know that this punishment is unjust, due to the deceit of this prophet of God, not to mention that the household was completely innocent? In Abraham's (pbuh) story, we are also told of Melchizedek, God's high priest who ministers to Abraham and brings with him "bread and wine" (14:18). The drinking of wine is not the kind of pass time you would think two men of God might partake in.

Abraham (pbuh) practiced polygamy just as Lamech had before him (4:23) and as most prophets did after him. He was an old man and his wife, Sarah was barren, but God had promised his offspring this land FOREVER (13:15). Sarah had a handmaid named Hagar. So Sarah "gave her (Hagar) to Abram her husband to be his wife (16:3). However Sarah began to feel animosity towards Hagar and she started to treat Hagar harshly (16:4-6, 21:10), to such an extent that Hagar ran away from Sarah. Hagar conceived a son named Ishmael (pbuh), meaning God hears, indicating that God heard and answered the prayers of Abraham (pbuh) (17:20) and the prayers of duress from Hagar (16:11). Though this is a named given to the child by God, there is also some disparaging news to be given. The angel tells Hagar to 'return to thy mistress, and submit thyself under her hands' (16:9). Even worse, the angel of God tells this new mother that her newborn son "shall be a wild ass of a man: his hand shall be against every man, and every man's hand against him; and he shall dwell in the face of all his brethren" (6:12). This again sounds like the author's prejudice or bias because we cannot sensibly attribute this insensitivity to God Almighty. He orders Hagar to return to her cruel mistress and even more bizarre is that he gives the mother the "good news" that her son with be an uncontrollable rebel against society. These are not very comforting words.

Even more interesting is despite the fact that Ishmael (pbuh) is the firstborn son, God defers the promised land to Abraham's (pbuh) second son, Isaac (pbuh), for no immediately apparent reason (17:18-19). God, at this point, changes Abram's (pbuh) name to Abraham (pbuh) (17:5). So God came to Abraham (pbuh) with two angels and they appeared as mortal men (18:1-2). Abraham (pbuh), showing his hospitality, had food prepared for them and they ate the food (18:5-8). Yes, God Almighty and 2 angels were served curd, milk and calf "and they did eat" in the Jewish Torah. They ate this meal and God told Abraham (pbuh) and Sarah, that he will return later and Sarah will have a son.

After giving this message, God and the angels set off to the land of Sodom and Gomorrah to determine whether or not to destroy its inhabitants. On the way to Sodom and Gomorrah, God and Abraham (pbuh) negotiate the fate of the people. Reluctant to have to explain his actions to Abraham (pbuh), God said or thought to himself "Shall I hide from Abraham that which I am doing" (18:17). Again God has come down to evaluate the situation himself and Abraham (pbuh) convinces God to pardon the people if God can find ten innocent people in the land (18:32). It becomes apparent with each story that God is believed to be only slightly wiser than his creation, yet less compassionate and understanding. He is described as being quite vengeful, yet fearful of his prophets' reactions. This is not the depiction of the perfect God in which most people envision.

Lot (pbuh)

After God is said to bargain with Abraham (pbuh) over the fate of the people of Sodom and Gomorrah, he disappears from the story and the reader is left with the 2 angels. They arrived in Sodom and they are greeted by Abraham's (pbuh) nephew Lot (pbuh). Lot (pbuh) prepared a feast for them and again "they did eat" (19:3). Perhaps they needed the strengthening and the rest to destroy the land. But before the angels could go to sleep, all the men of Sodom surrounded the house and shouted "bring them (the angels disguised as men) out unto us, that we may know them." I must stress that to "know" someone is used in this text to means "to have sex with." In an act of desperation, Lot (pbuh) offers the men his 2 daughters, who are married, yet he claims that they are virgins (19:8, 19:14). But this mob insisted upon going after the angels, who they thought were men. Such an egregious attempt was the last straw for God and he destroyed the people, including Lot's (pbuh) wife. Only Lot (pbuh) and his two daughters survived.

Lot's (pbuh) daughters believed him to be the last man on earth, so they got their father drunk with the ever-present wine and do the unthinkable. They both cohabited with their inebriated father (19:31-36). Now what is the point of such a story? God destroys a land of people for immoral behavior, but spares three individuals who soon after are perpetrators of incest, with absolutely no consequences or even a word of disapproval. Is this a story in which we are to teach our children? There really is no ground to stand upon in defense of this story, because this is not an act of necessity. This was not the entire earth that fell to God's wrath, but merely the land of Sodom and Gomorrah. The idea of such a story being inspired by God is unacceptable.

Also the sons produced by this incestuous relationship are named Moab meaning "from (her) father" and Ben-ammi meaning "son of my people or kinship." These names seem to intentional place a stigma on these two sons and their descendants, the Moabites and the Ammonites. But why? Perhaps the author had a hidden agenda. We shall revisit these people and maybe we will better understand why this story is told in this way.

Abraham's sons, Isaac and Ishmael (pbut)

21:1 And HaShem remembered Sarah as He had said, and HaShem did unto Sarah as He had spoken.

21:2 And Sarah conceived, and bore Abraham a son in his old age, at the set time of which G-d had spoken to him.

What did God do to Sarah for her to conceive a son? The language used here gives the skeptic the ammunition to attack this story. We know that there is nothing sinister here, but its narration leaves an opening for such an interpretation. This is an example of the callous manner in which some of the Jewish Torah is written. Its callous nature denotes the presence of human weakness or indifference.

Nonetheless, Sarah gives birth and she names her son, Isaac (pbuh). But she stills feels disdain for Hagar and her son, Ishmael (pbuh). She uses Ishmael's mocking of Isaac as an excuse to encourage Abraham (pbut) to send Hagar and her son away into the desert. Sarah says "the son of this bondwoman shall not be heir with my son" (21:10) and God beckons Abraham (pbuh) to follow his wife's instructions.

21:12 And G-d said unto Abraham: 'Let it not be grievous in thy sight because of the lad, and because of thy bondwoman; in all that Sarah saith unto thee, hearken unto her voice; for in Isaac shall seed be called to thee.

Now one may ask, is it not possible to grant Isaac (pbuh) the promise of the covenant without exiling an innocent women and her child into the desert? However God sees it fit to do such a thing in order to take Ishmael's birthright and give it to Isaac (pbut). Is mockery of a younger sibling grounds for exile? If so every older sibling on earth should be shipped to the desert. Why would God cater to the whims of a jealous woman? To add insult to injury, God begins to acknowledge Isaac as Abraham's "only son" (22:2) as if Ishmael (pbut) ceased to exist. This is the sign of human bias at work. There exists no practical or even a Biblical reason to exalt Isaac over Ishmael (pbut). According to Hebrew law, even if Hagar was a hated wife of Abraham (pbuh), but she conceived the first born, that child's rights are still upheld. As such the firstborn son inherits double of what the remaining children receive.

Deuteronomy 21:15 If a man have two wives, the one beloved, and the other hated, and they have borne him children, both the beloved and the hated; and if the first-born son be hers that was hated;
Deuteronomy 21:16 then it shall be, in the day that he causeth his sons to inherit that which he hath, that he may not make the son of the beloved the first-born before the son of the hated, who is the first-born;
Deuteronomy 21:17 but he shall acknowledge the first-born, the son of the hated, by giving him a double portion of all that he hath; for he is the first-fruits of his strength, the right of the firstborn is his.

The legitimacy of Ishmael's birthright has been challenged on numerous fronts by those who say Isaac is the true heir of Abraham (pbut), yet none can withstand scrutiny. Ishmael's mother has been called less than a pious woman, however the Jewish Torah testifies that she was Abraham's (pbut) wife and the law previously cited clearly allows for polygamy. There are no laws of the Jewish Torah which forbid polygamy, only those which regulate it (Ex. 21:10, Deut. 17:17, Deut. 25:5-10). There are some who suggest that because Hagar was Egyptian, that her and her child were not worthy of the promise of the land. This is nothing short of racism. Luckily, this argument is used very rarely. The idea of Hagar being a bondswoman is another means of assault of Ishmael's (pbuh) birthright. But as Ahmed Deedat once asked, "Is it better to marry a slave woman or your own sister?," because we do find that Abraham (pbuh) and Sarah were brother and sister (Gen. 20:12). This is yet another case of incest in this supposed book of God, and by a prophet of God, no less. If we consider the implications of Abraham (pbuh) and Sarah's incest, we would find that they are actually both cursed by God for this (Deut. 27:22) and their illegitimate offspring up to 10 generations are barred from entering God's assembly (Deut. 23:2). This means that Abraham, Sarah, Isaac and all of Isaac's (pbut) children are disqualified frombeing God's people, according to the law of the Jewish Torah.

These laws on the firstborn, marriage and incest are from the book of Deuteronomy and many people claim this to be laws formed after Abraham (pbuh) was on earth. However Abraham was also given laws and commandments to follow just as Moses (pbut) was (26:5). Are we to believe that God gave two different laws as it pertains to these issues? If we believe this to be the case, we are again left with the idea that God bends and twists his own law to aid in giving the birthright to Isaac (pbuh). This would be the only rational explanation as to why God would allow an innocent child to be stripped of his firstborn rights simply because his father's wife, Sarah, disliked the child's mother and Abraham's (pbuh) second wife, Hagar. Another point to be made is that the Jewish Torah continuously calls Ishmael Abraham's (pbut) son (16:15, 17:25, 25:12) despite people's opinion of him as being illegitimate and the scriptures saying Isaac is Abraham's "only son." The idea of multi-authors becomes more appealing in the sight of such blatant contradictions. This may also explain why Ishmael (pbuh) is not as far removed from the family as one may imagine, seeing that he and his mother live far off. When Abraham died, Ishmael assisted Isaac (pbut) in burying THEIR father (25:9).

ISAAC (pbuh)

25:5 And Abraham gave all that he had unto Isaac.
25:6 But unto the sons of the concubines, that Abraham had, Abraham gave gifts; and he sent them away from Isaac his son, while he yet lived, eastward, unto the east country.

Continuing the disdain for the Canaanite people, Abraham (pbuh) commands that Isaac (pbuh) not marry the daughter of a Canaanite (24:3). The life and wife of his other sons is unimportant to him, seeing that "he sent them away." It seems unlikely that such a caring father as Abraham (pbuh) was, he would have such favoritism for Isaac (pbuh) and such disinterest in his other children's lives. Nonetheless, the author would have us to believe that this strict heritage was not broken in accordance with Abraham's (pbuh) decree. So Isaac (pbuh) married a woman named Rebekah. And Isaac (pbuh) received all that Abraham (pbuh) had, including the proclivity of fooling the exact same king, Abimelech, with the same trick that his father pulled, saying that his wife was really his sister (26:9). Why exactly is this deceit from 2 men of God noteworthy in a book of God? From the standpoint of the Hebrew people, I would want to understand the significance of these events done by my forefathers, and why they warranted God's recollection? Nevertheless, Isaac (pbuh) and Rebekah are blessed with twin boys, who will be named Esau and Jacob (pbuh). And before they are born, God sheds some light on the future of these two sons.

25:23 And HaShem said unto her: Two nations are in thy womb, and two peoples shall be separated from thy bowels; and the one people shall be stronger than the other people; and the elder shall serve the younger.

Once again servitude is decreed to one sibling over another for no apparent reason, but let us look closer.

ESAU AND JACOB (pbuh)

Isaac (pbuh) had twin sons, Esau and Jacob (pbuh). Esau came out of the womb first despite Jacob (pbuh) grabbing his heel. This seems to give the impression that there is an inherit struggle between the twin brothers. And this theme plays out immediately in the Jewish Torah.

25:27 And the boys grew; and Esau was a cunning hunter, a man of the field; and Jacob was a quiet man, dwelling in tents.

In any great story we are provided with a protagonist and an antagonist. This very brief and general description of these two men seems to make this distinguish between the two brothers. However, the details of the story paint a very different picture. We are told that Esau, the outdoorsmen, came home famished one day and Jacob (pbuh) is cooking some stew. Naturally Esau asked his brother for a serving. However the "quiet man" refuses to feed his brother unless Esau promises to relinquish his firstborn birthright. The existence of this birthright is another testimony to the presence of a law preceding the laws given to Moses (pbuh). It would be more logical to assume that the laws were first written down by Moses, and not revealed to Moses first, as it appears that laws written in the Jewish Torah were being adhered to long before Moses (pbuh) existed. But let us get back to the story.

25:32 And Esau said: 'Behold, I am at the point to die; and what profit shall the birthright do to me?'
25:33 And Jacob said: 'Swear to me first'; and he swore unto him; and he sold his birthright unto Jacob.
25:34 And Jacob gave Esau bread and pottage of lentils; and he did eat and drink, and rose up, and went his way. So Esau despised his birthright.

It is obvious the Esau believed that he will die if he does not eat and his brother saw him in this vulnerable state and capitalized on it. Jacob (pbuh) seems to be aware of the benefits of being the first born, so he bribes Esau into relinquishing possession of this right. What is peculiar is that Genesis' author declares that it is reasonable to believe that Esau "despised his birthright" from this episode. The word "so" in verse 34 indicates that Esau's disdain for the birthright is personified in a story in which he is, whether in reality or in his own mind, starving to death and his twin brother victimizes him. His actions, at the most, would signify his presumptuousness about starving to death and his unwillingness to accept death as an alternative to giving away his birthright. I would assume that Esau felt the way many rational people do today, that decisions made under duress are not lawful or even acceptable to another rational person, let alone God. The author intends for the reader to understand that Esau had such contempt for the firstborn right that he gave it away for a plate of food, therefore he did not deserve it in the first place and Jacob's (pbuh) actions are insignificant. And this goal would have been achieved had the author not recorded Esau's sincere belief that he was "at the point to die." Yet the story continues.

First we find that Esau marries two outsiders, Hittite women. And Hittite women are grouped with Canaanite women, which mean they are off limits to Abraham's descendants. Thus Esau and his wife, Judith, "were a bitterness of spirit unto Isaac (pbuh) and to Rebekah" (26:34-35). We read from their inception, that Isaac and Rebekah chose their favorites between the two sons. "Now Isaac loved Esau, because he did eat of his venison; and Rebekah loved Jacob" (25:2). Esau is not short of enemies. His brother is after his birthright, Isaac (pbuh) and Rebekah's racism have turned them against their son and the author of Genesis, who speaks for God, seems to have it out for Esau.

Despite Isaac's (pbuh) disapproval of Esau's wife, Isaac still plans to give his elder son the firstborn's blessings before he dies. He beckons Esau to make him a dish, so he can give Esau this final blessing. Esau heads out to the fields to hunt for food for this dish. It is obvious that Esau is determined to receive this blessing. However, his mother has a different idea. Rebekah overheard this conversation between Isaac (pbuh) and Esau and she conspires to steal this blessing from her son, Esau and give it to her beloved son, Jacob. Isaac (pbuh), on his deathbed, was "old and his eyes were dim, so that he could not see" (27:1). Disregarding her husband's condition and his conviction, she devises a plan which would take advantage of Isaac's (pbuh) ailment. She instructs Jacob (pbuh) to get two kid goats, so she can make a savory meal and Jacob (pbuh) will act as though he is Esau, give the meal to Isaac (pbuh), and get the blessing. However Jacob (pbuh) is greatly concerned with how this trick can be pulled off because Esau was a hairy man and Jacob (pbuh) was not and Isaac (pbuh) may become aware of their scheme and curse Jacob (pbuh). But Rebekah takes care of this.

27:13 And his mother said unto him: 'Upon me be thy curse, my son; only hearken to my voice, and go fetch me them.'
27:14 And he went, and fetched, and brought them to his mother; and his mother made savoury food, such as his father loved.
27:15 And Rebekah took the choicest garments of Esau her elder son, which were with her in the house, and put them upon Jacob her younger son.
27:16 And she put the skins of the kids of the goats upon his hands, and upon the smooth of his neck.

Even though Isaac (pbuh) is a bit suspicious, the plan works. Rebekah's meal, the skins of the goat to make Jacob (pbuh) hairy, Isaac's (pbuh) blindness, Esau's struggle to bring back his father's meal, and the ever-present WINE for Isaac (pbuh) combine to bring about the results Jacob (pbuh) and Rebekah most passionately desired. But what of poor Esau? Just as Jacob (pbuh) steals the blessings and leaves his father, Esau, who was at least 40 years old at the time (26:34), comes in to see his father, after laboriously hunting and preparing a dish, in utter disbelief. So too was Isaac (pbuh).

27:33 And Isaac trembled very exceedingly, and said: 'Who then is he that hath taken venison, and brought it me, and I have eaten of all before thou camest, and have blessed him? yea, and he shall be blessed.'
27:34 When Esau heard the words of his father, he cried with an exceeding great and bitter cry, and said unto his father: 'Bless me, even me also, O my father.'
27:35 And he said: 'Thy brother came with guile, and hath taken away thy blessing.'
27:36 And he said: 'Is not he rightly named Jacob? for he hath supplanted me these two times: he took away my birthright; and, behold, now he hath taken away my blessing.' And he said: 'Hast thou not reserved a blessing for me?'
27:37 And Isaac answered and said unto Esau: 'Behold, I have made him thy lord, and all his brethren have I given to him for servants; and with corn and wine have I sustained him; and what then shall I do for thee, my son?'
27:38 And Esau said unto his father: 'Hast thou but one blessing, my father? bless me, even me also, O my father.' And Esau lifted up his voice, and wept.
27:39 And Isaac his father answered and said unto him: Behold, of the fat places of the earth shall be thy dwelling, and of the dew of heaven from above;

27:40 And by thy sword shalt thou live, and thou shalt serve thy brother; and it shall come to pass when thou shalt break loose, that thou shalt shake his yoke from off thy neck.

I can only reproduce the reactions of Isaac (pbuh) and Esau, because its impact cannot be duplicated by my words. The vision of an elderly men violently shaking as he tells his son, who has spent the day hunting for game and preparing the meal, that his work was in vain, is vividly expressed in these verses. Esau's pleading to have some small blessing is heartfelt. We also see the benefits that go with the firstborn rights and blessings. Jacob (pbuh) is now Esau's lord and Esau must serve him. Esau must live by the sword, which is similar to the proclamation that Ishmael (pbuh) shall have "every man's hand against him," while his brother enjoys a much easier life. The question is, "where is God in this story?"

It appears that God allows such actions as beguiling your elderly blind father with the aid of your mother, because he makes no attempt to overturn this injustice. He makes special trips to earth to see things for himself, but he does not right this wrong. Perhaps he condones this because according to the Jewish Torah, Esau was predestined by God to be a servant to Jacob (25:23). In this story, Rebekah is willing to pull out all the stops in order to get this blessing, including garner the punishment if her plan fails. Rebekah, like Sarah and Eve before her, persuades her husband to do as she wishes, which in each case is morally wrong. Yet Eve is the only one who is admonished for her actions. And since God did not condemn the acts or Sarah and Rebekah, we must ask, are their actions permissible in the sight of God? Rebekah is quoted as saying to Isaac (pbuh):

27:46 "'I am weary of my life because of the daughters of Heth. If Jacob take a wife of the daughters of Heth, such as these, of the daughters of the land, what good shall my life do me?'

She considers her life worthless, if her beloved son marries outside of his race. Isaac (pbuh) is also warned not to marry the Canaanite women (24:3). Only poor Esau is race and colorblind. But he being already married to 2 Hittites, tries to please his father by marrying an Ishmaelite (28:8-9), probably making matters worse.

JACOB (pbuh)

At this time, Rebekah has informed Jacob (pbuh) that Esau is so bitter that he is seeking to kill Jacob (pbuh) for stealing his blessing. So Jacob (pbuh) flees for his life. On his journey, he runs into the daughter of his uncle Laban, Rachel. He wastes no time in his efforts to get close to Rachel. He helps her with her sheep "and Jacob (pbuh) kissed Rachel, and lifted up his voice, and wept" (29:11). Rachel runs away and tells her father what happened. Laban embraces his nephew, gives him shelter and a job. Jacob (pbuh) asks for Rachel's hand in marriage in exchange for his services. But what is interesting is how the author prefaces Jacob's request. Not Jacob, but the "godly" inspirations of the author reveal that the oldest sister was not very attractive but the younger sister, Rachel was of beautiful form and fair to look upon (29:17). So Jacob (pbuh) worked for seven years for Rachel to be his wife. When the seven years were up, the crude Jacob (pbuh) went to Laban and said plainly,

29:21 'Give me my wife, for my days are filled, that I may go in unto her.'

Laban, unfazed by these crass words, gave Jacob (pbuh) BOTH of his daughters. The end of chapter 29 and all of chapter 30 simply describe the virile Jacob (pbuh) and his various wives with whom he begot 11 sons, Reuben Simeon, Levi, Judah, Dan, Naphtali, Gad, Asher, Issachar, Zebulun, Joseph (pbuh) and a daughter named Dinah. With the birth of another son, Benjamin and the story of Jacob's (pbuh) name change, the reason behind these biases and immoral acts attributed to God and men of God in Genesis start to manifest.

JACOB (PBUH) TO ISRAEL

In my opinion the most startling and outlandish story in the Jewish Torah and in the entire Bible is the story of Jacob's (pbuh) name change. Seeing that the name Israel is mentioned various times in the news, in conversation, and in every reading of the Jewish Torah, it is amazing to me that this name change is not considered a noteworthy topic.

The scene is of Jacob (pbuh) on the run from his brother, Esau. Jacob (pbuh), in the middle of the night, took his wives and maid servants over the ford of Jabbok and he sent them over a stream.

32:25 And Jacob was left alone; and there wrestled a man with him until the breaking of the day.
32:26 And when he saw that he (the man) prevailed not against him (Jacob), he (the man) touched the hollow of his (Jacob's) thigh; and the hollow of Jacob's thigh was strained, as he(the man) wrestled with him (the man).
32:27 And he (the man) said: 'Let me go, for the day breaketh.' And he (Jacob) said: 'I will not let thee go, except thou bless me.'
32:28 And he said unto him: 'What is thy name?' And be said: 'Jacob.'
32:29 And he said: 'Thy name shall be called no more Jacob, but Israel; for thou hast striven with G-d and with men, and hast prevailed.'

32:30 And Jacob asked him, and said: 'Tell me, I pray thee, thy name.' And he said: 'Wherefore is it that thou dost ask after my name?' And he blessed him there.
32:31 And Jacob called the name of the place Peniel: 'for I have seen G-d face to face, and my life is preserved.'
32:32 And the sun rose upon him as he passed over Peniel, and he limped upon his thigh.
32:33 Therefore the children of Israel eat not the sinew of the thigh-vein which is upon the hollow of the thigh, unto this day; because he touched the hollow of Jacob's thigh, even in the sinew of the thigh-vein.

Please take a moment to soak this story in. Now take another moment. With all due respect, the objective of this book is fulfilled completely with this story. As a teenager, my mother brought this story to my attention and I was baffled at its presence in a book claiming to be the words of God. If you have not figured out why I am outraged by this story, allow me to explain. The man in which Jacob (pbuh) is wrestling is GOD ALMIGHTY. GOD ALMIGHTY, GOD ALMIGHTY! The Jewish Torah contains a multitude of questionable characteristics of God, but this example epitomizes them all. There is absolutely no sensible reason for this story's existence. The Jewish Torah says that Jacob (pbuh) was alone, so there were no eyewitnesses.

The only persons who could convey this story was Jacob (pbuh) and God. And who would believe a man wrestled God all night and PREVAILED. Most assuredly God would not document the defeat of his might and power by a mere mortal. There have been attempts to change the character in this story to an angel, however you can flip this story inside out and there is not one mention of an angel. But we do have the author's testimony that Jacob (pbuh) saw God "face to face." Perhaps Jacob (pbuh) did not know that Abraham (pbuh) had already seen and fed God (pbuh), but he did know that it was a miracle that he saw God and his "life was preserved." Thus he named the place where he wrestled God, Peniel, which means "the face of God." It is clear that Jacob (pbuh) knew that "no man can see god and live" (Ex. 33:20) long before Moses (pbuh) came with this truth, which again establishes the fact that laws were given before Moses (pbuh) had his.

If we closely evaluate the story, we find that God initiates the fight and even utilizes his supernatural power to injury Jacob's (pbuh) thigh but God remains subdued and unable to escape Jacob's (pbuh) clutches. He asks Jacob (pbuh) to "let him go." Of course, Jacob (pbuh), sensing that this is no ordinary man, goes after more blessings. This is the very thing that had him on the run in the first place. Apparently Jacob's (pbuh) blessing was his name change. God asks Jacob (pbuh) what his name was, and then he changed his name to Israel. Jacob (pbuh) inquiries about the name of the man which he is wrestling, but God does not give his name (This may be the inception of the idea that God's name is not to be spoken). So as a result of this wrestling match which placed Jacob (pbuh) against God and the whole of mankind, he is to be called Israel. Here lies the truth of the matter, Israel literally means "to wrestle with God."

Isra- to grapple with
El- God

Recently I read the book, "Purpose Driven Life" by Rick Warren and to my astonishment, the author of this book acknowledges plainly that Jacob wrestled GOD ALMIGHTY, GOD ALMIGHTY, GOD ALMIGHTY, and this book is a best seller. Everywhere I went holding this book in hand, someone asked me about it and they explained how their church had study groups about this book. Yet not one of them saw any problem with the idea that a human being defeated the Supreme Being in which they worship. The same is true for the Jewish believers of the Jewish Torah in which I have encountered. Because this is a sensitive, but significant topic, I must not stop short of my evidence to support my position. As I have stated, several people have claimed that an angel wrestled Jacob. Some go so far as to title the story, "Jacob wrestles an angel" in order to sway the reader into understanding an alternate view from what is so plainly visible. The author of the book of Hosea makes such a claim.

12:3 In the womb he supplanted his brother: and by his strength he had success with an angel.
12:4 And he prevailed over the angel, and was strengthened: he wept, and made supplication to him: he found him in Bethel, and there he spoke with us.

Even in this case, there exists a great problem. The problem is that God has sent this angel and Jacob (pbuh) defeats him, thus God is still defeated, just as a military defeat is the defeat of the general. With this said, we see the author's real intention is to build a story and legend around Israel (Jacob). That Israel, like the nation in which he spawns, will go against "God and men and prevail." It seems the author of Hosea saw the need to rectify the stance that Jacob (pbuh) made because it is clear that Jacob (pbuh) said this man was God, not an angel. In fact, "angels of God" are mentioned in the beginning of the chapter in Genesis which contains the altercation, thus differentiating them from this "man" (32:1). In Hosea's haste, he failed to consider "God's" words on this altercation. In chapter 35 of Genesis, we find ample evidence from God's mouth that this was indeed God that Jacob (pbuh) wrestled, just as the author of the story records and as Jacob (pbuh) understood.

35:1 And G-d said unto Jacob: 'Arise, go up to Beth-el, and dwell there; and make there an altar unto G-d, who appeared unto thee when thou didst flee from the face of Esau thy brother.'
35:7 And he built there an altar, and called the place El-beth-el, because there G-d was revealed unto him, when he fled from the face of his brother.

But what is strange is that the multiple author argument rears its head again, when God changes Jacob's (pbuh) name to Israel for a second time.

35:9 And G-d appeared unto Jacob again, when he came from Paddan-aram, and blessed him.
35:10 And G-d said unto him: 'Thy name is Jacob: thy name shall not be called any more Jacob, but Israel shall be thy name'; and He called his name Israel.

Even more strange is that after telling Jacob (pbuh) twice that his name is no longer Jacob(pbuh), but Israel, God and the author call him Jacob (pbuh) again and again (42:36, 46:2, 46:5).

In conclusion, this cannot be the words of God, for this story is in direct contradiction to the nature of God and his inability to lose to his own creation, no matter their strength or conviction. This is a very serious matter and a believer in the Jewish Torah should consider the implications of such a story. In my estimation this is the final piece of the puzzle. It is proof that the Jewish Torah is not the words of God, but a morale booster for the children of Israel. Its author begins with his take on the creation of the world and peers through the opposite side of a funnel to the inception of Israel, totally ignoring or disregarding the existence of any other people. And the author gives God this narrow-mindedness as well.

If this book is the words of God, then he has an affinity for no other people but the children of Israel. I believe at this point, it is apparent that the Jewish Torah is not the words of God, if any of these claims that I made are true. But I would like to take you on a journey just to see to what extent the author of the Jewish Torah will go to proclaim the children of Israel's greatness. I want the reader to envision the purpose of man's life on earth, to ponder every thought surrounding our existence in this universe and to consider the benefits of following God's words and let us see if the Jewish Torah gives us these answers.

Now the summation of the story of Esau and Jacob (pbuh) is found in the book of the prophet Malachi. In this book we find something quite interesting. Despite all the lies and cheating and wrestling of Jacob (pbuh),

God professes his loves for him. And despite the hardships Esau faced at the hands of his brother and his forgiveness of Jacob (pbuh) for those hardships (33:4), GOD HATED Esau. I have heard and read a number of explanations or apologies for this passage but none are sufficient. The only reason that one might love the sinner and hate his victim is HUMAN FAVORITISM. If you read the Hebrew Scriptures upside down or backwards it still will not account for this:

Malachi 1:2 I have loved you, saith HaShem. Yet ye say: 'Wherein hast Thou loved us?' Was not Esau Jacob's brother? saith HaShem; yet I loved Jacob;
Malachi 1:3 But Esau I hated

BILHAH AND REUBEN

35:22 And it came to pass, while Israel dwelt in that land, that Reuben went and lay with Bilhah his father's concubine; and Israel heard of it. Now the sons of Jacob were twelve...

When reading this verse in the Jewish Torah, one can easily read over this story without fully understanding what has happened. Reuben is Israel's son and Bilhah is Israel's wife. These two had sexual relations. Some may suggest that Bilhah was not Israel's wife, but his concubine, as if this provides any justification to the event. Though it says that she is his concubine in this verses, it is apparently customary to refer to a man's wife as a concubine in the Jewish Torah. Bilhah was Israel's first wife Rachel's maid (29:29) and one of Jacob's "concubines" (35:22), but she also was called his "wife," both before and after she gave birth to two of

Jacob's sons (30:4; 37:2). Bilhah was not Reuben's mother. However one would think that upon hearing the news that his son and his wife had committed incest, Israel might have had something to say about it. But Israel and the author of the Jewish Torah care little about this egregious sin. It is of such little regard to both of them that they make no effort to denounce such an act. The author makes no note of Israel's response and the telling of the lineage of Israel continues unabated. Israel "heard" about it and that is all. Would God or a prophet of God inspire such a story to be told in his book without admonition! Without admonition, the telling of such a story seems to promote the actions as permissible or at least inconsequential.

DINAH DEFILED

The one daughter amongst the 12 sons of Israel was Dinah. There is very little written about her aside from the incident in which she is "humbled."

34:1 And Dinah the daughter of Leah, whom she had borne unto Jacob, went out to see the daughters of the land.
34:2 And Shechem the son of Hamor the Hivite, the prince of the land, saw her; and he took her, and lay with her, and humbled her.

The word used here is "humbled." Some translators use the words "ravished", "violated", "raped", "defiled" or "lay with her by force." However the use of the word "humbled" intrigued me, because it is so tame compared to the other translations. There is a dispute as to whether Dinah and Shechem had consensual relations or not and the word "humbled" only adds to the dispute. Even the word "defiled" could cause this incident to have a less provocative understanding. Shachem is in love with Dinah and he asks his father, Hamor, to speak to Dinah's father, Jacob (pbuh) (though his named was supposedly changed to Israel, the author still calls him Jacob), about Shechem marrying Dinah. It seems to be a bit audacious for a rapist to make such a request, involving his victim and her father no less.

34:5 Now Jacob heard that he had defiled Dinah his daughter; and his sons were with his cattle in the field; and Jacob held his peace until they came.
34:6 And Hamor the father of Shechem went out unto Jacob to speak with him.
34:7 And the sons of Jacob came in from the field when they heard it; and the men were grieved, and they were very wroth, because he had wrought a vile deed in Israel in lying with Jacob's daughter; which thing ought not to be done.

It appears that the defilement of Dinah has to do with the fact that Shechem is amongst those groups in which children of Israel cannot marry. The words “which ought not be done” suggests that this is the case because it goes without saying that a rape “ought not be done.” Nonetheless Shechem is insistent upon marrying Dinah. He asks Jacob (pbuh) could he marry her for any dowry and gift. But the sons of Jacob (pbuh) said “We cannot do this thing, to give our sister to one that is uncircumcised; for that were a reproach unto us.” They contend that if Shechem and every man among his people are circumcised, they will give him their sister’s hand in marriage.

Not only did they offer Dinah to be his wife but they said “we give our daughters unto you, and we will take your daughters to us, and we will dwell with you, and we will become one people.” Shechem and all the Hivite men happily consented. They said

34:21 "These men are peaceable with us; therefore let them dwell in the land, and trade therein; for, behold, the land is large enough for them."

Completely unlike the uncompromising logic of the children of Israel and "God," the Hivites were eager to coexist with the children of Israel and share everything they had with them.

34:25 And it came to pass on the third day, when they were in pain, that two of the sons of Jacob, Simeon and Levi, Dinah's brethren, took each man his sword, and came upon the city unawares, and slew all the males.
34:26 And they slew Hamor and Shechem his son with the edge of the sword, and took Dinah out of Shechem's house, and went forth.
34:27 The sons of Jacob came upon the slain, and spoiled the city, because they had defiled their sister.
34:28 They took their flocks and their herds and their asses, and that which was in the city and that which was in the field;
34:29 and all their wealth, and all their little ones and their wives, took they captive and spoiled, even all that was in the house.

Some might say that Shechem did not rape Dinah, but this is only an opinion, but even if he had, the repercussions were completely unjust. Punishing the guilty is not a crime, but killing these innocent men who were already "in pain" and stealing their wives and children and even their livestock is a crime and a sin. What did they do with their wives?

What did they do with their children? One might be in great anticipation of how God will rectify this injustice. God, according to the Jewish Torah, said not one word in admonition to the sons of Jacob (pbuh) for this atrocity. What did their father, a man of God, say to his sons about this crime? At that moment, Jacob (pbuh) seems too preoccupied with the repercussions of his neighbors to show his disdain for the actions done by these men in whom God shows so much favor. But to Jacob's (pbuh) credit, later he does denounce his sons' treachery and punishes them as well.

49:5 Simeon and Levi are brethren; weapons of violence their kinship.
49:6 Let my soul not come into their council; unto their assembly let my glory not be united; for in their anger they slew men, and in their self-will they houghed oxen.
49:7 Cursed be their anger, for it was fierce, and their wrath, for it was cruel; I will divide them in Jacob, and scatter them in Israel

But this is not the last time the Jewish Torah records such cruelty perpetuated by the children of Israel, and there will be no denouncement by any man of God, or by God. In fact, it appears that God may endorse this kind of behavior done by his people.

JUDAH AND TAMAR

One of the children of Israel named Judah, from which the terms Judaism, Jewish and Jew comes from, goes and marries a Canaanite women whose name is mysteriously omitted.

38:2 "and he took her, and went in unto her."

Is it necessary to describe the act which is required to conceive a child? Would it not be more fitted to simply state that they got married and had children. This kind of uncouth speech is repeated frequently in the Jewish Torah and especially as it pertains to sex. The words "went in unto her" give the reader a mental picture which is not required at all in this instance. But this is the tip of the iceberg. Judah and the daughter of Shua had three sons, Er, Onan, and Shelah. Judah found a wife for his first born, Er, and her name was Tamar.

38:7 And Er, Judah's first-born, was wicked in the sight of HaShem; and HaShem slew him.
38:8 And Judah said unto Onan: 'Go in unto thy brother's wife, and perform the duty of a husband's brother unto her, and raise up seed to thy brother.'
38:9 And Onan knew that the seed would not be his; and it came to pass when he went in unto his brother's wife, that he spilled it on the ground, lest he should give seed to his brother.
38:10 And the thing which he did was evil in the sight of HaShem; and He slew him also.

This story is not for the faint of heart. Do we declare that God inspires man to scribe in such a lewd manner? Can this moral point be conveyed without the explicit details? There are children's books based on the tales of the Jewish Torah. Does this story qualified as a story in which children should study or even come in any contact with? It draws a lewd picture of their dealings with Tamar and a harsh God, who considers people worthy of death for this particular sin. Does this "one strike and you're out" law apply to Judah?

Judah's wife died and he was in great mourning. After this period of mourning was over, he went to a place called Timnah to shear his sheep. Throughout this time, Tamar was waiting for Judah's youngest son, Shelah, to grow up so she could marry him. Her patience began to wear thin, when Tamar saw that Shelah had become a grown man and he had not married her yet. In Moses' (pbuh) law, if a brother dies without having children from his wife, his brother must give her children for the deceased brother (Deut. 25:5). Again we see that this law was in effect long before Moses (pbuh) had it implemented. It seems that Judah had enough of his sons dying in an effort to fulfill this law and he decided to spare his son, Shelah, from falling victim to God's wrath, if he fell short of the goal. So, Tamar decides to take matters into her own hands. She heads towards Timnah and stops at its entrance waiting for Judah to see her with a veil covering her face.

38:15 When Judah saw her, he thought her to be a harlot; for she had covered her face.
38:16 And he turned unto her by the way, and said: 'Come, I pray thee, let me come in unto thee'; for he knew not that she was his daughter-in-law. And she said: 'What wilt thou give me, that thou mayest come in unto me?'

Judah offers Tamar, his daughter-in-law, a kid from his flock and he gives her his signet and cord as a guarantee of payment. Judah "came in unto her, and she conceived by him" (38:18). Later, Judah came back with the kid looking for the "harlot" but the townspeople said that no harlot was in that town. Three months later, Judah is given the news that Tamar, his son's widow, was pregnant. Knowing that he did not give Shelah to be her husband, Judah commands that she be brought to him and he says "let her be burnt." (38:24). There seems to be no inkling of consideration for the twins in her stomach. However, Tamar has a trump card. She says the father is the owner of the "signet and cord" that she possesses. Judah, out of guilt, exonerates Tamar. She is released and gives birth to twins, Perez and Zerah (38:29-30).

That is the end of this story of Judah and Tamar. There is no punishment or correction by God. What is the moral to this story? It is a story one might want to keep far away from a child or even a sensitive adult. It seems to have no place in a book of God. And Judah is far removed from a person in whom any honor should be bestowed. He is also said to have suggests that his younger brother Joseph (pbuh) be sold into slavery (37:26-27), yet the religion of Judaism gets its name from this man.

Add this to the stories already mentioned. God's chosen seed of Abraham (pbuh) and their infractions are well documented and enumerated in the first book of the Jewish Torah alone. As we recall, Abraham (pbuh) questions God's decision making earlier in the scripture. It leads the reader to question God's decision to choose such sinful people or it calls into question God's authorship of this book.

JOSEPH (pbuh)

What would call for more questioning is the idea that the author seems confused about certain matters, like to whom Joseph (pbuh) is sold. Joseph (pbuh), one of the few Israelites who seems to be worthy of praise in the Jewish Torah, had a dream that he would rule over this brothers. Joseph's (pbuh) brothers resented him because he was Israel's (37:3) or Jacob's (37:1-2) favorite child, not to mention the fact that Joseph (pbut) "brought an evil report of them (his brothers) unto their father" (37:2). His dream only incited more anger towards himself and intrigue from the reader as to why God insists upon contradicting his own firstborn law, as Joseph (pbuh) was to rule over his brothers even though he was not the firstborn son. (Could this law be unjust to begin with?) Nonetheless, his brothers wished to kill him for his dream. Judah, however, says instead of killing him, they should sell him to the Ishmaelites (37:26-27), as he saw a group of them passing by. It appears that the Midianites were passing by at the very same time (37:28). The brothers, the Ishmaelites, and the

Midianites crossing each other all at once, maybe confuses the author of the Jewish Torah. First he says that the brothers sold Joseph to the Midianites, who then sold Joseph to the Ishmaelites (37:28), but in the very same chapter, we read that the Midianites had him captive and sold him in Egypt to "Potiphar, an officer of Pharaoh's, the captain of the guard" (37:36). The problem is accentuated when we read

39:1 And Joseph was brought down to Egypt; and Potiphar, an officer of Pharaoh's, the captain of the guard, an Egyptian, bought him of the hand of the Ishmaelites, that had brought him down thither.

This kind of mistake is a human error and should not be attributed to God as his words or his inspiration. Judah recommends selling Joseph (pbuh) to the Ishmaelites, but he never does. The Midianites came and rescued Joseph (pbuh) out of the pit that his brothers threw him in. Then they sold him either to the Ishmaelites or to Potiphar. There are those who contend that the author is merely using the words, Ishmaelite and Midianites, interchangeably. This response is not completely thought through, because this only shifts the problem, making it appear that the author cannot differentiate between two groups of people, one being the descendants of Ishmael (pbuh) and the other being the children of his brother, Midian. The author can certainly differentiate between them and their brother, Isaac (pbuh) and his offspring. It seems that the Jewish Torah's author is suggesting that these groups are of such insignificance that it is of no consequence if they are lumped together. Yet the offspring in which the Jewish Torah glorifies offer very little in terms of models of the God-fearing. Whichever position you take, it remains a far cry from what God would have inspired.

As I cite incidents such as God continuously calling Israel, "Jacob," after insisting twice that his name is Israel and yet another case of firstborn rights overruled, when Joseph (pbuh) defers the right to his youngest son

(48:14-20), I must reiterate that my goal in this book is to give examples of why I believe the Jewish Torah is not the words of God. This is not to say that there is no lesson to be learned from the Jewish Torah or that great truths are not present in these books. The knowledge and wisdom contained in these books have been documented throughout the centuries. I am simply proposing that the presence of truth is not the sole grounds for declaring a book to be from God, neither is the absence of falsehood. The book must pass every test of validity and the examples in which I cite, in my opinion fall short of passing the tests of validity. The arguments that I have cited above are the grounds on which I declare that the 1st book of the Jewish Torah is not the word of God.

EXODUS

The remaining books of the Jewish Torah focus on the prophet Moses (pbuh), his brother Aaron (pbuh) and the children of Israel's pursuit of God's Promised Land. In the book of Exodus, we begin to see more frequently the appearance of God's favoritism for the Israelites. God refers to them as "my people" (3:10) and he refers to himself as "the God of the Hebrews" (3:18). In Exodus, we find the Israelites in subjection to the Egyptians. This inevitably made the Egyptians to believe themselves superior to the Israelites. The Egyptians thought it beneath them to eat with the Hebrews. The author of the Jewish Torah, knew this beforehand, so he mistakenly placed the pronouncement that "Egyptians eating with Hebrews is an abomination" in the times of Joseph (pbuh) (Gen. 43:32). This must have been a mistake because, when Joseph (pbuh) was in Egypt, he was the only Hebrew there. And all the other Hebrews were Joseph's (pbuh) family, who lived in Canaan. So it is impossible for the Egyptians to have formed this decree, if they never encountered the Hebrews. The author placed this rule in a time hundreds of years before it would have been in effect. Surely God would not make such an error. This might also explain the ill treatment of God, Sarah and Abraham (pbuh), to the Hagar, a supposed Egyptian handmaid and her son. The author belittles them because of the Egyptians' harsh treatment of those whom the Jewish Torah is gear towards, later on in history.

SLAVERY

The book begins with the children on Israel put into slavery by the Egyptians and their king. Apparently there is word of a liberator to be born to the Hebrew people, who will emancipate the Israelites from this bondage. This liberator was to be the first born son of a Hebrew family. Therefore the Egyptian pharaoh decrees that all the male children of the Hebrews be killed (1:16). The idea of such an evil act is abhorrent. The hope of continuing one's domination by means of killing an innocent child, with no regard for their life or the parent's grief, is unimaginable. Yet this very act in which we see as wicked becomes completely acceptable when it is said that God does the exact same thing to the Egyptians.

MOSES (pbuh) IS BORN

Moses' (pbuh) mother, a Hebrew, is aware of the pharaoh's plans so she hides Moses (pbuh) for 3 months, until it becomes impossible to hide him any longer. She put him in an ark and pushed him out into the river (2:3). He is discovered by the pharaoh's daughter and she takes him as her son (2:9-10). Just as Joseph (pbuh), an Israelite, was indistinguishable from the Egyptians when he lived amongst them (He was the only Hebrew in Egypt, yet his own brothers could not recognize him. Gen. 42:8), so too was Moses (pbuh) indistinguishable from the Egyptians as he is received as the grandson of the pharaoh.

The narrative shifts into gears and we read that Moses (pbuh) is a grown man and he identifies with his people's plight as slaves. And he happens to come upon an Egyptian man beating a Hebrew.

2:12 And he looked this way and that way, and when he saw that there was no man, he smote the Egyptian, and hid him in the sand.

The fact that he is described as casing out the scene insinuates premeditation to a crime. Then he proceeds to kill the Egyptian and hide his body. A man prone to such behavior seems ill fit for godly duties. However, God chooses this man, Moses (pbuh), to deliver his message to the pharaoh.

MOSES' (pbuh) CALLING/GOD'S NAME

After hearing about the killing of the Egyptian, the pharaoh orders Moses (pbuh) to be killed. So Moses (pbuh) flees to Midian. There he met and lived with a man named Reuel (2:18-21) who gave Moses (pbuh) his daughter Zipporah's hand in marriage. Strangely in the next chapter, Reuel is now called Jethro. As Moses (pbuh) is looking after Jethro's sheep, an angel of God appears to Moses (pbuh) as a burning bush. Presumably through the angel, God commands Moses (pbuh) to go to the pharaoh and tell the pharaoh to free the children of Israel from slavery. The children of Israel, having felt the agony of slavery, prayed to God for a deliverer. Now was the time for the deliverer to send God's message, "Let My People Go!"

Moses (pbuh) agrees to deliver the message but he wants to be able to tell the pharaoh the name of the God that sent him.

3:14 And G-d said unto Moses: 'I AM THAT I AM'; and He said: 'Thus shalt thou say unto the children of Israel: I AM hath sent me unto you.'

The thing that interests me is that "I am that I am" doesn't seem to be a name at all, but rather a gesture to show that the importance of God's name in this instance is secondary to the message in which Moses (pbuh) must deliver. Or it may be an attribute for which God can be called. It is a universal belief that God is eternal, having no beginning or ending and "I am that I am" might satisfy this attribute of God. There are profound explanations to the "name" given, but any layman who came upon this verse without outside influence would not take this as a literal name. The fact that God shortens the name, to "I am," is added support to this position because it is unlikely that God has a nickname.

3:15 And G-d said moreover unto Moses: 'Thus shalt thou say unto the children of Israel: HaShem, the G-d of your fathers, the G-d of Abraham, the G-d of Isaac, and the G-d of Jacob, hath sent me unto you; this is My name for ever, and this is My memorial unto all generations.
3:16 Go, and gather the elders of Israel together, and say unto them: HaShem, the G-d of your fathers, the G-d of Abraham, of Isaac, and of Jacob, hath appeared unto me, saying: I have surely remembered you, and seen that which is done to you in Egypt.

If the aforementioned title is God's name, then this passage only casts more confusion to the reader. The words "I am that I am" in Hebrew are *ehyeh asher ehyeh* and "I am" is *ehyeh*. One peculiar point is that in verse 12 of the same chapter in question, *ehyeh* is translated "I will be" but two verses later the translation on the same word changes to "I am." The difference between present and future tense is very significant, changing the phrase to "I will be that I will be." However in verse 15, HaShem or "The Name" is a replacement for the Hebrew tetragammaton which occurs in the original Hebrew Scriptures as *YHWH*. These four letters are written without the vowels because in Judaism, God's name is forbidden to be spoken. The word *ehyeh* and *YHWH* derive from the root word *hayah* meaning "to be." However these are obviously two different words, thus different names are recorded for God within one verse of each other. *Ehyeh* (I am) is the first person form, whereas *YHWH* (He is) is the third person form of the root "to be." I would suggest that "I am" or "I will be" and "He is" are not names but attributes of God. They are used to demonstrate to Moses (pbuh) and his listeners that the message is what is to be focused upon. In fact, verse 15 should read "He is God of your father, God of Abraham, God of Isaac and God of Jacob." The problem, aside from continuing to call Israel by the name Jacob (pbuh), is that God is speaking these words to Moses (pbuh) and if the third person form (*YHWH*) is sacred, why is the first person form (*Ehyeh Asher Ehyeh*) permissible to speak?

What is amazing is that this topic is not brought up at all when Moses (pbuh) is confronting the pharaoh or when he is with the Israelites. I am inclined to believe that entire episode stems from the confusion of its author. The author, who is traditionally identified as Moses (pbuh), is writing in third person throughout the remainder of the Jewish Torah and he records that God never told anyone his holy name before Moses (pbuh).

6:3 and I appeared unto Abraham, unto Isaac, and unto Jacob, as G-d Almighty, but by My name YHWH made Me not known to them.

Yet Abraham (pbuh) and his wife Sarah call God by this name on numerous occasions (Gen. 12:8, 13:4, 21:33). In fact, the name *YHWH* occurs about 160 times in the book of Genesis. Jacob told his father Isaac (pbut), that *YHWH* "thy God" aided him in his endeavors (Gen. 27:20). Therefore God is wrong or the author is incorrect in putting this name on anyone's lips before Moses (pbuh). Later in the book of Exodus, we find another "name" for God, which makes it clear that these are attributes of God.

34:14 For thou shalt bow down to no other god; for HaShem, whose name is Jealous, is a jealous G-d

GOD'S ANGER

In any case, Moses (pbuh) receives a response to his question, but he has reservations about going to speak to the pharaoh because he had a speech impediment. In a discussion with Moses (pbuh) about speaking with the pharaoh, "the anger of HaShem was kindled against Moses, and He said: 'Is there not Aaron thy brother the Levite?'" (4:14). It would seem that God can't have a disagreement with someone without being angry. God tells Moses (pbuh) that he is in control of people's speech, hearing and understanding. Of course he is correct, but getting upset over an argument is not a good example to follow. Of all the things going on in the universe, it appears that the slightest event can send God into a rage, such as a speech impaired man afraid of ridicule. Is this how we are to deal with those who we wish to overcome their affliction? What is strange is that God sets aside his first argument, that he can control his speech impediment, and quickly hands the duty to Moses' brother Aaron (pbut) THE LEVITE. Is this the remedy to help Moses (pbuh)? Probably not. And what is the author of Exodus trying to emphasize by stressing that Aaron is a Levite? Is Moses not a Levite also? This may be similar to the emphasis used when describing Ham as "the father of Canaan." We shall see.

GOD SEEKS TO KILL MOSES (pbuh)

4:21 And HaShem said unto Moses: 'When thou goest back into Egypt, see that thou do before Pharaoh all the wonders which I have put in thy hand; but I will harden his heart, and he will not let the people go.
4:22 And thou shalt say unto Pharaoh: Thus saith HaShem: Israel is My son, My first-born.
4:23 And I have said unto thee: Let My son go, that he may serve Me; and thou hast refused to let him go. Behold, I will slay thy son, thy first-born.'

I begin with this quote of God giving Moses (pbuh) instructions in order to paint the picture of the setting of this strange sequence of events. Moses (pbuh) is to tell the pharaoh to let his people go, but the pharaoh's rejection of this command is a foregone conclusion, because God will make this so by "hardening his heart" (7:3, 10:27, 11:10). God also declares that Israel is his first-born son. If he means Jacob (pbuh) or all of the Israelites, it is confusing how Israel became his first-born son. Jacob (pbuh) was not the first person to believe in God, not to mention the fact that he wrestled and defeated God. There were the sons of God spoken of even before Noah (pbuh). And there were people who believed in God before the term Israel was pronounced. Even more bizarre is that on another occasion, God says "for I am a father to Israel, and Ephraim is my firstborn" (Jer. 31:9). In Jeremiah, it seems that God is speaking of two individuals or groups, but the problem is that Israel is Ephraim's grandfather and God was with Israel long before Ephraim's own father, Joseph (pbuh) was born, so it is impossible for Ephraim to be the first born.

In any case, God continues to tell Moses (pbuh) that he wants Israel to be free, so they can worship him and if the pharaoh does not free them, then God will kill his first born. We already know that God will make pharaoh reject this command because God will cause him to reject it, but this would mean that God has intentions on killing innocent children. Is this the God in which we envision as merciful and just? That withstanding, Moses (pbuh) must have left this conservation with God feeling encouraged and ready to go. Little did he know that he was also on the list for God's "mercy."

4:24 And it came to pass on the way at the lodging-place, that HaShem met him, and sought to kill him.
4:25 Then Zipporah took a flint, and cut off the foreskin of her son, and cast it at his feet; and she said: 'Surely a bridegroom of blood art thou to me.'

4:26 So He let him alone. Then she said: 'A bridegroom of blood in regard of the circumcision.'

From the words conveyed here, I conclude that God was about to kill Moses (pbuh) simply because Moses' (pbuh) son was not circumcised. Perhaps, a disagreement between Moses (pbuh) and God about this uncircumcised child was too heinous a crime to be overlooked. Even if that were the case, could not God warn his chosen prophet, as he does the pharaoh on numerous occasions, before he issues punishment. The word "kill" in this verse insinuates a malicious intent. We normally consider God taking someone's life as a natural occurrence, but for God to "kill" someone seems to signify a definite evil which must be extinguished. The sons of Judah, Er and Onan, were wicked and evil in the sight of God so he killed them. Moses (pbuh) is described as a premeditated murderer and refuge from justice, yet these acts are not considered evil at all. Perhaps this is because it was not an Israelite who was harmed, but an Egyptian. Or maybe assault of an Israelite justifies premeditated murder. Not only is this murder justifiable or ignorable, but it qualifies Moses (pbuh) to be a prophet of God, yet fear and non-circumcision warrants God to personally seek and kill someone.

10 PLAGUES

Zipporah saves her husband and God sends Moses (pbuh) as a God to pharaoh (7:1), telling him to let God's people go. Of course, the pharaoh's heart is hardened by God and he refuses to release the Children of Israel. It appears God has hardened the pharaoh's heart in order to show his might over the pharaoh. God hardens the pharaoh's heart and he prescribes 10 different plagues of punishments for this disobedience.

1. rivers turned to blood (7:14-25)
2. frogs (7:26-8:11)
3. lice (8:12-15)

4. swarm of insects (8:16-28)
5. disease on livestock (9:1-7)
6. skin boils (9:8-12)
7. hail mixed with fire (9:13-35)
8. locusts (10:1-20)
9. darkness (10:21-29)
10. God killed the firstborn of Egypt (11:1-12:36)

The first plague was when Aaron struck the rivers with his rod and then all the water turned to blood. The problem here is that Exodus says that the magicians performed the same feat as Moses and Aaron (pbut) did. How did they also turn water into blood when Aaron (pbuh) had already contaminated all the water in the area for seven days (7:14-25)? And the plague of the locusts is said to have covered the FACE OF THE WHOLE EARTH (10:15). Was everyone on earth held responsible for the crimes of the Egyptians? That is a lot of locusts! Perhaps the author exaggerated a bit. But the worse plague was the last one, the killing of all the firstborn of Egypt. God killed the innocent firstborn child of the Egyptians, but how was this is to be carried out? Though "HaShem doth put a difference between the Egyptians and Israel" (11:7), the author of Exodus suggests that God cannot understand his own distinction, because the Children of Israel were very much susceptible to the "killing of the firstborn" by God had they not followed specific instructions. The Israelites were to kill a lamb and use its blood to mark their homes, to be an indicator to God Almighty whose homes he must pass over, so he won't make a mistake and kill the wrong children (12:3-13). Perhaps the distinction God put between them was this lamb's blood. This does nothing to explain why the all-knowing God is in need of such a distinction. Nonetheless, the Passover is commemorated every year by the followers of Judaism.

12:29 And it came to pass at midnight, that HaShem smote all the firstborn in the land of Egypt, from the first-born of Pharaoh that sat on his throne unto the first-born of the captive that was in the dungeon; and all the first-born of cattle.

12:30 And Pharaoh rose up in the night, he, and all his servants, and all the Egyptians; and there was a great cry in Egypt; for there was not a house where there was not one dead.

GODS

In the book of Exodus, we see that God is called "the God of the Israelites." Moses (pbuh) is to tell the Israelites God's words, "I will take you to Me for a people, and I will be to you a G-d" (6:7), so they can worship him (4:23, 5:1, 8:1, 9:1). Notice that there appears to be an acceptance of other gods, i.e, "a God" or "there is none like unto HaShem our G-d" (8:6 or 8:10). Is this henotheism?

God is referred to on numerous occasions as the "God of the Hebrews" (3:18, 5:3, 7:16), which suggests that other gods exist. After God's handling of the pharaoh, Jethro, Moses father-in-law, is convinced "that HaShem is greater than all gods" (18:11). God, himself, is said to have left the door open for other gods as he declares, "Thou shalt have no other gods before Me," in what is commonly called the Ten Commandments. Even more peculiar is that Moses (pbuh) describes God as a "MAN of war." Some translations may read "the Master of war" but the Hebrew word "*Rashi*" is literally "man."

15:3 HaShem is a man of war, HaShem is His name.

The phrase "man of war" gives the impression that God has an inclination towards war instead of peace; this only strengthens the problem that God is described as a man. If we consider the stories told in Genesis of a regretful, vengeful being who indulges in earthly food, debate and struggles, it is not a far stretch to conclude that this God is a man. Not to mention, the Jewish Torah says that he rested after creation. The argument over God resting, as described in Genesis, has been challenged by Jews and Christians, alike. They contend that the word "rest" only means to cease from work. However, they forget that Moses (pbuh) or whoever wrote the Jewish Torah explained in greater detail that God did literally rest after making creation. If this is not the case, then what are we to understand from 31:17 in which we read "On the seventh day, He rested and was refreshed." And in Genesis 2:2, it is already stated that he "ended his work," therefore when it says he rested, it must have been a recuperation process.

Genesis 2:2 And on the seventh day God ended his work which he had made; and he rested on the seventh day from all his work which he had made.

The Jewish Torah is riddled with sightings of God (Gen. 12:7, Ex. 6:3, 19:11, 24:9-11), as well as face to face dialogue with God (Gen.32:30). Moses (pbuh) spoke with God "mouth to mouth" (Num. 11:17, 12:8) and he is said to have been a lucky recipient of a "face to face" with God (Ex.33:11, Num. 14:14). Yet we read that Moses (pbuh), in the very same chapter of Exodus, asked to see God. The result of seeing God had been known to Jacob and God reiterates this consequence to Moses (pbut).

33:20 And He said: 'Thou canst not see My face, for man shall not see Me and live.'
33:21 And HaShem said: 'Behold, there is a place by Me, and thou shalt stand upon the rock.
33:22 And it shall come to pass, while My glory passeth by, that I will put thee in a cleft of the rock, and will cover thee with My hand until I have passed by.

33:23 And I will take away My hand, and thou shalt see My back; but My face shall not be seen.'

From this dialogue, I understand that no one can see God and live. God must pass by Moses (pbuh) in this circumstance and in order to do this without taking Moses' (pbuh) life, God placed Moses (pbuh) in a cleft in a rock, and he covers the rock with his "hand" so Moses (pbuh) couldn't see his "face." When God removed his "hand" Moses (pbuh) saw God's "back." The sight of God's back is later described as seeing the likeness of God (Num. 12:8). There is such a thing as anthropomorphism in religious literature used figuratively to convey a certain message. But this anthropomorphism seems to be used literally to convey a certain message. "This God is a Man."

GOD AND THE CHILDREN OF ISRAEL

Following the 10th plagues, God finally softened the pharaoh's heart. Amidst the great mourning from Egypt, pharaoh told Moses (pbuh) to gather all the Israelites and take them away to serve their God. And the Israelites were freed from 430 years of slavery. With their newfound freedom came ordinances such as all males are to be circumcised (12: 44-50) and the firstborn is to be dedicated to God (13:1-2). And of course, God reminds them of their promised land. But God was not done with the pharaoh.

14:4 "And I will harden Pharaoh's heart, and he shall follow after them; and I will get Me honour upon Pharaoh, and upon all his host; and the Egyptians shall know that I am HaShem."

God again hardened the pharaoh's heart and he pursued Moses (pbuh) and the Israelites. As a wondrous miracle, God splits apart the Red Sea or the Sea of Reeds, so the Israelites may pass through it. The pharaoh and his men follow behind the Israelites, but God closes the passage through the sea and the Egyptians and the pharaoh are drowned.

14:31 And Israel saw the great work which HaShem did upon the Egyptians, and the people feared HaShem; and they believed in HaShem, and in His servant Moses.

Yet despite the marvels they witnessed and the fear and belief they proclaimed, the Israelites were extremely ungrateful for all that God and Moses (pbuh) had done for them. They acquired a habit of preferring their past condition of slavery over their conditions of freedom. They continuously insisted that God brought them out of bondage only to have them die in the wilderness (14:11-12). They also murmured against God for their hunger (16:3-7). They were even ready to kill Moses (pbuh) because they were thirsty.

17:4 And Moses cried unto HaShem, saying: 'What shall I do unto this people? they are almost ready to stone me.'

This ungratefulness, unfaithfulness and impatience beg the question, why did God chose these people? Their behavior has Moses (pbuh), an obvious man of strength, crying in disillusion to God for help and in fear of his life. Of course, God's motives are not our own, but God displays great power and might against the Egyptians for the pharaohs disbelief, so how can he exalt another people for a similar and possibly greater disbelief? The Egyptians were said to have worshipped the animals that the Hebrews sacrificed to God (8:22 or 8:26). Was the Israelites belief in the God of Abraham, Isaac and Jacob (pbut) enough to grant them distinction from all other groups on earth, even if they considered God inept on occasion?

GOLDEN CALF

The Israelites fell victim to idol worship, as well. While Moses (pbuh) was away on Mount Sinai in the presence of God, the Israelites were amazingly asking his brother Aaron (pbuh) to make them a golden calf to worship. They said “make us a god who shall go before you” (32:1) and Aaron (pbuh) conceded. All the people gathered their golden earrings.

32:4 And he received it at their hand, and fashioned it with a graving tool, and made it a molten calf; and they said: 'This is thy god, O Israel, which brought thee up out of the land of Egypt.'
32:5 And when Aaron saw this, he built an altar before it; and Aaron made proclamation, and said: 'To-morrow shall be a feast to HaShem.'

Aaron (pbuh) and these stiff-necked people (32:9) were first hand witnesses to God’s power, yet they proclaimed a calf, in which they assembled, to be the God that saved them from the pharaoh.

32:10 Now therefore let Me alone, that My wrath may wax hot against them, and that I may consume them; and I will make of thee a great nation.'
32:11 And Moses besought HaShem his G-d, and said: 'HaShem, why doth Thy wrath wax hot against Thy people, that Thou hast brought forth out of the land of Egypt with great power and with a mighty hand?

32:12 Wherefore should the Egyptians speak, saying: For evil did He bring them forth, to slay them in the mountains, and to consume them from the face of the earth? Turn from Thy fierce wrath, and repent of this evil against Thy people.
32:13 Remember Abraham, Isaac, and Israel, Thy servants, to whom Thou didst swear by Thine own self, and saidst unto them: I will multiply your seed as the stars of heaven, and all this land that I have spoken of will I give unto your seed, and they shall inherit it for ever.'

We find God beseeched with enough anger to wipe out all those who took the golden calf as God to be worshipped. But as Abraham does in Genesis, Moses (pbut) rationalizes with God. In fact, he says if you kill these people, the Egyptians would mock the Israelites delivery from bondage. Is this how we arrive at justice? Does God defer punishment based on the perceptions of idolatrous slave owners? Even more strange is that despite the constant mention of the promise to the Israelites by God, it is he who must be reminded of this promise by Moses (pbuh), in order to calm GOD ALMIGHTY down. Is this promise to the Israelites unconditional? We shall see. However Moses (pbuh) asks GOD ALMIGHY to kindle his wrath and repent from "EVIL" (32:14). Moses (pbuh), a prophet of God, declares God's thoughts to be evil. Can God commit evil or sinful deeds? Apparently in the Jewish Torah, he can.

After counseling God, Moses (pbuh) comes down from the mount in such a rage that he throws down and breaks the stone tablets, on which God has engraved the Ten Commandments. He also grinded the golden calf into powder, stewed the powder in water and made the Israelites drink it. Yet this is not enough for the rational Moses (pbuh). After having Aaron explains what happened, Moses (pbut) does something unexpected.

32:27 And he said unto them: 'Thus saith HaShem, the G-d of Israel: Put ye every man his sword upon his thigh, and go to and fro from gate to gate throughout the camp, and slay every man his brother, and every man his companion, and every man his neighbour.'

According to this narrative the Levites were the only group with the good sense to serve the God which freed them. So Moses (pbuh) instructs them to gather swords and go from gate to gate and kill "every man his brother, and every man his companion, and every man his neighbour." Even though God was counseled by Moses (pbuh) not to kill the sinners because he and Moses (pbuh) both rendered this an evil act, both were responsible for the deaths of 3,000 Israelites (32:28).

32:35 And HaShem smote the people, because they made the calf, which Aaron made.

LAWS

It may seem that God intended to kill all of the Israelites for the sins of those 3,000, but if we look closely at the details after the mass killing we find that Moses (pbuh) offers himself as a sacrificial lamb for the sins of Israel, but God says he only punishes those that has sinned against him (32:32-33). It is obvious that the author of Exodus has committed a grave error when he writes that God only punishes the sinner because we find the exact same circumstance of worshipping other Gods as the Hebrews did and God decrees, in the commonly named Ten Commandments, that it will be detrimental to the CHILDREN of those Israelites who partake in the worship of other gods.

20:3 Thou shalt have no other gods before Me.
20:4 Thou shalt not make unto thee a graven image, nor any manner of likeness, of any thing that is in heaven above, or that is in the earth beneath, or that is in the water under the earth;
20:5 thou shalt not bow down unto them, nor serve them; for I HaShem thy G-d am a jealous G-d, visiting the iniquity of the fathers upon the children unto the third and fourth generation of them that hate Me;
20:6 and showing mercy unto the thousandth generation of them that love Me and keep My commandments.

As with the worship of the golden calf, the words "no other gods before me" has led many to believe that the Israelites were henotheists and their adherence to strict monotheism came after their encounter with Zoroastrianism during the Babylonian capture. This idea is very plausible when we consider that the Hebrew Scripture contains many stories of the Israelites worshipping many other gods besides the one true God, until you get to the books of the prophets like Isaiah, who vehemently denies the existence of any god but one. After the Babylonian capture, there is never again any reference to other gods in which the Israelites worshipped.

Verse 4 of chapter 20 seems to condemn the practices of artists and photographers as well as those who serve any being or figure depicted in art or photography. The reason being is that God is JEALOUS of these other figures being worshipped, besides or along with him. This human emotion of jealousy seems incorrect to attribute to God. He deserves all praise, but does it hurt his feelings or make him envious to have mankind worship another god? Even more ungodly is the notion that if you are amongst those who take others for worship beside the one true God, he will punish their innocent children and their children's children to the fourth generation and bless the righteous' children through thousands of generations. This is where Christians assemble the idea that sin and its punishments are inherited. This idea is purely unjust and no civilized court in the world operates in this manner. Can we suppose that God would punish the innocent for the iniquities of their parents? Yet this is exactly want is said in the commandments. Though not in the Jewish Torah, we do find rectification of this proposed punishment of the innocent in Ezekiel chapter 18.

18:20 The soul that sinneth, it shall die; the son shall not bear the iniquity of the father with him, neither shall the father bear the iniquity of the son with him; the righteousness of the righteous shall be upon him, and the wickedness of the wicked shall be upon him.
18:21 But if the wicked turn from all his sins that he hath committed, and keep all My statutes, and do that which is lawful and right, he shall surely live, he shall not die.
18:22 None of his transgressions that he hath committed shall be remembered against him; for his righteousness that he hath done he shall live.

It is clear here that we are not responsible for others sin, but our own sin. In the same vein, we are not righteous simply because our parents were righteous. God judges man by their individuals deems, whether sinful or saintly. This sentiment is found in the conversation noted earlier between Moses (pbuh) and God, in which God says he will punish those who have sinned against him, not an innocent person. Thus the author of Exodus gives God conflicting views on the penalty of sin within chapters of each. Can punishment for inherited sin and punishment for only the guilty party both be principles of God?

DEATH PENALTY

It is impossible to believe in the Hebrew Scriptures and be opposed to the death penalty. The laws of the Jewish Torah are to be adhered to by the Israelites and many of them are enforced with dire consequences. For instance, it says "honor your mother and father" (20:12), but if you strike either of them, you are to be put to death (21:15). Amazingly insulting your parents garners the exact same punishment as assaulting them (21:17). Understandably murder, conspiracy to commit murder (21:12, 14) and kidnap (21:16) (an offense perpetrated by ten of the children of Israel) are capital offenses but is cursing your parents just as heinous. Working on the Sabbath is another crime punishable by death (31:15-17). God is so adamant about man resting as he did on the last day of the week that he repeats this punishment in chapter 35:2. What about religious tolerance and apostasy in the laws of the Jewish Torah? These two are categorized with having sex with an animal.

22:17 Thou shalt not suffer a sorceress to live.
22:18 Whosoever lieth with a beast shall surely be put to death.
22:19 He that sacrificeth unto the gods, save unto HaShem only, shall be utterly destroyed.

What is the fate of those peoples who worship other gods beside the "God of the Hebrews"? According to the Jewish Torah, God leaves no hint of or room for reconciliation when he commands the Israelites to "break down their altars, and dash in pieces their pillars, and ye shall cut down their (non-Israelites) Asherim" (34:13). Of course the Amorite, the Hittite, the Perizzite, the Canaanite, the Hivite, and the Jebusite had no idea reconciliation was necessary until their sacred churches were destroyed. Perhaps they had no idea because they performed no infractions upon the Israelites, other than believing in a God different from the Israelite's God.

23:23 For Mine angel shall go before thee, and bring thee in unto the Amorite, and the Hittite, and the Perizzite, and the Canaanite, the Hivite, and the Jebusite; and I will cut them off.
23:24 Thou shalt not bow down to their gods, nor serve them, nor do after their doings; but thou shalt utterly overthrow them, and break in pieces their pillars.
23:27 I will send My terror before thee, and will discomfit all the people to whom thou shalt come, and I will make all thine enemies turn their backs unto thee.
23:28 And I will send the hornet before thee, which shall drive out the Hivite, the Canaanite, and the Hittite, from before thee.
23:29 I will not drive them out from before thee in one year, lest the land become desolate, and the beasts of the field multiply against thee.
23:30 By little and little I will drive them out from before thee, until thou be increased, and inherit the land.
23:31 And I will set thy border from the Red Sea even unto the sea of the Philistines, and from the wilderness unto the River; for I will deliver the inhabitants of the land into your hand; and thou shalt drive them out before thee.
23:32 Thou shalt make no covenant with them, nor with their gods.
23:33 They shall not dwell in thy land--lest they make thee sin against Me, for thou wilt serve their gods-for they will be a snare unto thee.

OTHER LAWS AND PENALTIES

The laws of the Jewish Torah were known to Moses (pbuh) long before they were written down. Probably due to their enslavement, it was necessary for them to reestablish the law. Moses (pbuh) used these laws to judge in cases between the Israelites (16:28). With the huge number of people to judge, the task became impossible for one person to handle, so Moses (pbuh) appointed judges to give judgments in most cases and he would handle only the major cases. These laws were in effect since the times of Abraham but Moses (pbut) now decides to write them down (24:4). In reading these words, we find no first person reference to Moses (pbuh) and no acknowledgment that these are the exact words in which Moses (pbuh) wrote. The prevalence of the Hebrew heritage throughout the Jewish Torah, like 6:14-25, suggests that this book is meant for the history of Israelites and not the whole of humanity. Perhaps this is a book which is used to inspire self esteem in light of the tremendous trials Israelites faced throughout history. This is a noble cause, but nobility can't be synonymous with godliness in this instance, when we consider the implications of the errors and injustices purported to be dictated by God.
Such examples include the regulations placed upon a man selling his daughter into slavery (21:7-11) or the law that a slave's wife and children belonging to his slave master, if the slave master was responsible for introducing the couple (21:2-4). The idea of slaves being the master's property is a great cause for concern.

21:20 And if a man smite his bondman, or his bondwoman, with a rod, and he die under his hand, he shall surely be punished.
21:21 Notwithstanding if he continue a day or two, he shall not be punished; for he is his money.

Would God consider slaves to be property? What about thieves? We find that if you kill a burglar there is no punishment, but if he lives and he has no money or property for restitution for his crime, God allows you to sell him (22:1-3). Thus a slave and a thief have similar worth according to the Jewish Torah.

We have all heard the law “an eye for an eye” and “a tooth for a tooth” (21:24), but most of us have never read or heard the law that follows this one. It pertains to the penalty given for smiting the eye or tooth of a slave.

21:26 And if a man smite the eye of his bondman, or the eye of his bondwoman, and destroy it, he shall let him go free for his eye's sake.
21:27 And if he smite out his bondman's tooth, or his bondwoman's tooth, he shall let him go free for his tooth's sake.

For certain, the person enslaved would much rather be free than to reciprocate the injury in which he suffered, but this law begs the question,“Is this the method in which slaves are freed?” There are also laws for paying taxes in which the poor are commanded to pay the same taxes as the rich. Even more amazing is that the rich are directly told not to exceed the fixed amount and the poor are not to give less than the fixed amount. “They give the offering of HaShem, to make atonement for your souls” (35:11-16). This sounds like a tax given by man, which does not take into account the hardships of the poor and the ease at which the rich can pay this tax. Would not God take into account that a poor man’s dollar bill is of far greater value to him than a rich man’s dollar bill is to him? The story of Cain and Abel’s offerings to God, gives a better insight into the more justifiable viewpoint, which we may ascribe to God.

Abel’s offering is said to be “the firstlings of his flock and of the fat thereof” (Gen. 4:4) and Cain’s offering is not described at all. God respected Abel’s offering, but he did not respect Cain’s. God’s lack of respect along with the absence of the details of Cain’s offering implies that it was less than Cain’s best (Gen. 4:67). In like manner “half a shekel” from a poor man is far greater than a rich man’s “half a shekel.” It seems the author was looking out for the interest of the rich and not that of the poor, which does not seem very godly.

REAFFIRMATION

The PROMISE is reiterated on numerous occasions but it cannot be stated enough that this promise has a prerequisite which must be established and continued in order to acquire and maintain the land.

19:5 Now therefore, if ye will hearken unto My voice indeed, and keep My covenant, then ye shall be Mine own treasure from among all peoples; for all the earth is Mine

However, it appears that the people chosen and distinguished from all other people had little intentions of ever actually following the laws which they were given. And because of their heedlessness, God wishes to kill them again. He cannot be in their presence for an instant lest he wipes them off the earth.

33:2 and I will send an angel before thee; and I will drive out the Canaanite, the Amorite, and the Hittite, and the Perizzite, the Hivite, and the Jebusite-
33:3 unto a land flowing with milk and honey; for I will not go up in the midst of thee; for thou art a stiff-necked people; lest I consume thee in the way.'

33:4 And when the people heard these evil tidings, they mourned; and no man did put on him his ornaments.
33:5 And HaShem said unto Moses: 'Say unto the children of Israel: Ye are a stiffnecked people; if I go up into the midst of thee for one moment, I shall consume thee; therefore now put off thy ornaments from thee, that I may know what to do unto thee.'

These are the people in whom he is said to give an abundance of forgiveness and grace (Ex.34:9-10, Num. 14:19). Yet he offers no forgiveness or even guidance but punishment to those people who inhabit the Promised Land.

LEVITICUS

GOD

The book of Leviticus is mainly rules and regulations that the Israelites are to live by. It does contain some aspects of Moses' and Aaron's (pbut) life as well. But I am more concerned with the possibility that it is in fact God dictating these laws and stories about his prophets and himself. For instance, Leviticus on numerous occasions mentions God smelling pleasant fragrances, described as a "sweet savour to God" (2:2, 2:9, 3:5). I would assume that this is metaphoric and not literal, for God actually smelling burnt offerings would be far-fetched, despite the numerous anthropomorphic images given to him. Many translators make it difficult to come to this conclusion when they use words such as "odors pleasing to God." But it is crystal clear that God has a special affinity for the children of Israel.

The power of suggestions is a tremendous tool. Leviticus repeats over and over again, "Your God" (11:44-45, 18:2, 4,19, 19:24,10,12,14,31-32,34,36, 25:36-38, 26:13). What effect might this have on a people? If this God proves himself superior to the gods of the others, these two words becomes an immediate seed for racism. How could you possibly think of yourselves as anything but superior to everyone else who are not a part of God's people, especially when you are rebellious and God continues to bless you and punish others? There is no passageway set for others to become one with you. Not once is there any mention of conversion for the non-Israelite or the non-Israelites following the laws to become a part of the chosen people. In fact, there are to be two sets of laws made, one for the homeborn Israelites and another set for strangers (Lev. 24:22). If this is the case, then even conversion is not enough to make you a part of the chosen people, unless you happen to be born in the "right" place at the "right" time. And these laws had to be separate and "unequal" because according to the Jewish Torah, God has already distinguished and chose Israelites above the "strangers." These laws cover every aspect of life, down to the food they eat. God instructed them to abstain from eating or even touching swine (11:1-8), abstain from things of the sea without fins or scales (11:12), and blood of animals, etc. Failure to follow such laws resulted in the violator being "cut off" from his people (7:25-27).

DIVISIVE LAWS

The laws of the Jewish Torah seem to distinguish between men and women, as well. Of course, there are obvious distinctions but when it comes to the burnt offerings to God, we read that "every male among the priests may eat thereof; it is most holy" (6:22, 7:6). The man is privileged to eat of the burnt offering in this case, conspicuously omitting "every female among the priests." This may be due to "God's" perception of woman as being unclean or at least making their mother as such.

12:1 And HaShem spoke unto Moses, saying:
12:2 Speak unto the children of Israel, saying: If a woman be delivered, and bear a man-child, then she shall be unclean seven days; as in the days of the impurity of her sickness shall she be unclean.
12:3 And in the eighth day the flesh of his foreskin shall be circumcised.
12:4 And she shall continue in the blood of purification three and thirty days; she shall touch no hallowed thing, nor come into the sanctuary, until the days of her purification be fulfilled.

12:5 But if she bear a maid-child, then she shall be unclean two weeks, as in her impurity; and she shall continue in the blood of purification threescore and six days.

The author of Leviticus purports that God made female birth double the amount of impurity (14 and 66 days) for the mother than that of a male child (7 and 33 days). Of course, science is in complete disagreement with "god" in this matter. In fact, male children are more likely to pass away at or before child birth than female children, not to mention that women's lifespan far exceeding men's lifespan. This would also seem to contradiction the notion that women are less pure than men. In any case, God could not have inspired these words attributed to him. What is interesting is the words this translator used. In a possible attempt to camouflage this problem of sexism, he translates the words "maid-child", when most translators use the words "female child" or "girl" which seems to be the proper translation in this case. A maid can be defined as "an unmarried girl or woman" or "a virgin", but this passage is in reference to an infant, therefore these definitions are given facts. Also common reference of a maid in English is in reference to a servant, so using the words "maid-child" only compounds the problem, giving the reader the understanding that female children are maids from birth. Further and rather explicit evidence of the significance of a male over that of a female is personified in Leviticus which seemingly places a dollar value on each group.

27:1 And HaShem spoke unto Moses, saying:
27:2 Speak unto the children of Israel, and say unto them: When a man shall clearly utter a vow of persons unto HaShem, according to thy valuation,

27:3 then thy valuation shall be for the male from twenty years old even unto sixty years old, even thy valuation shall be fifty shekels of silver, after the shekel of the sanctuary.
27:4 And if it be a female, then thy valuation shall be thirty shekels.
27:5 And if it be from five years old even unto twenty years old, then thy valuation shall be for the male twenty shekels, and for the female ten shekels.
27:6 And if it be from a month old even unto five years old, then thy valuation shall be for the male five shekels of silver, and for the female thy valuation shall be three shekels of silver.
27:7 And if it be from sixty years old and upward: if it be a male, then thy valuation shall be fifteen shekels, and for the female ten shekels.

There are also laws ostracizing those with diseases. Of course, the fear of the spread of a disease has always been a part of human society, but it seems unsympathetic and cruel for God to make the leper rip his clothes apart, uncover his head, cover his upper lip and scream out that he is "UNCLEAN, UNCLEAN!!!" (13:45)

WINE

God specifically tells Aaron (pbuh) not to drink wine or any strong drink (10:8-9) in order to distinguish himself as clean and holy, unlike the unclean commoners. Aaron must have a clear head in order to teach the laws of Moses (pbut). The problem with this is that despite the numerous sins committed in conjunction with wine, this law is not for the whole of the Israelite people. When we consider that God describes those that drink wine or strong drink as unclean common people, it is strange that God would not make this a universal rule. Also are those men of God, who indulged in alcohol, unholy or unclean?

LAWS ABOUT RELATIONSHIP

There are numerous laws describing who the Israelites are not allowed to be involved with in a relationship, but the one which struck me to be unjust is the one in which a man "takes his brother's wife." The law stipulates that this is incest and the couple is to be childless (20:21). I understand this as a sin, but I do not understand the punishment. It is obvious that in almost all instances the couple will be able to conceive a child and without the use of contraceptives in that time period, babies will be born to this couple. So how does God suggest making them childless? The options are a crude surgery, abstinence, adoption or abortion. The author may have known the Israelites reluctance to carry out this punishment, so he follows it with a threat.

20:22 Ye shall therefore keep all My statutes, and all Mine ordinances, and do them, that the land, whither I bring you to dwell therein, vomit you not out.

Homosexuality is called an abomination in which you are defiling yourself by its indulgence (18:22), though the penalty is not recorded until two chapters later along with other acts of sexual immorality.

20:10 And the man that committeth adultery with another man's
wife, even he that committeth adultery with his neighbour's wife,
both the adulterer and the adulteress shall surely be put to death.
20:11 And the man that lieth with his father's wife--he hath
uncovered his father's nakedness--both of them shall surely be put
to death; their blood shall be upon them.
20:12 And if a man lie with his daughter-in-law, both of them
shall surely be put to death; they have wrought corruption; their
blood shall be upon them.
20:13 And if a man lie with mankind, as with womankind, both of
them have committed abomination: they shall surely be put to
death; their blood shall be upon them.
20:14 And if a man take with his wife also her mother, it is
wickedness: they shall be burnt with fire, both he and they; that
there be no wickedness among you.
20:15 And if a man lie with a beast, he shall surely be put to death;
and ye shall slay the beast.
20:16 And if a woman approach unto any beast, and lie down
thereto, thou shalt kill the woman, and the beast: they shall surely
be put to death; their blood shall be upon them.

God shows no mercy in his prescribed punishment for these sins, but some appear a bit excessive, like killing the animal involved. Speaking of capital punishment, insulting your parents (20:9) and being possessed by spirits (20:27) are also punishable by death. Those Israelites who chose to turn from their God and worship Molech were to be stoned to death, as well (20:2-3). Also if the daughter of a priest performs sexual immoral acts, she is to be burned to death (21:9).

There was a man who was the son of an Israelite mother and an Egyptian father. He cursed using the name of God. Those who heard this brought him before Moses (pbuh). Moses (pbuh) declared that all of the congregation must stone the fellow (24:1023) and they stoned him to death. Moses (pbuh) even said the "foreigners" who blasphemy the name of God are to be stoned to death. Is this a law which could and should be established today?

CONSEQUENCES

We are reminding that the God of the Jewish Torah is swift in his wrath, when he took the lives of his Prophet Aaron's (pbuh) two sons for offering a "strange fire" to God (10:1-2). They did not make an offering to a strange god, they offered a "strange" fire to their God. So God sent his own fire down on the two sons of Aaron (pbuh) and it devoured them. Perhaps the strange fire is one which is offered to strange gods, and God took offense to it and killed them both.

Apart from the threat of death for violations of the law, God promises even greater punishment as long as the transgressors live, perhaps to make them long for death. If they do not hearken unto God, if they reject his statutes, if they abhor his ordinances and they will not do all these commandments (Lev. 26:14-15), a rash of penalties will besiege them.

26:16 I also will do this unto you: I will appoint terror over you, even consumption and fever, that shall make the eyes to fail, and the soul to languish; and ye shall sow your seed in vain, for your enemies shall eat it.

26:17 And I will set My face against you, and ye shall be smitten
before your enemies; they that hate you shall rule over you; and ye
shall flee when none pursueth you.
26:18 And if ye will not yet for these things hearken unto Me, then
I will chastise you seven times more for your sins.
26:19 And I will break the pride of your power; and I will make
your heaven as iron, and your earth as brass.
26:20 And your strength shall be spent in vain; for your land shall
not yield her produce, neither shall the trees of the land yield their
fruit.
26:21 And if ye walk contrary unto Me, and will not hearken unto
Me; I will bring seven times more plagues upon you according to
your sins.
26:22 And I will send the beast of the field among you, which
shall rob you of your children, and destroy your cattle, and make
you few in number; and your ways shall become desolate.
26:23 And if in spite of these things ye will not be corrected unto
Me, but will walk contrary unto Me;
26:24 then will I also walk contrary unto you; and I will smite
you, even I, seven times for your sins.
26:25 And I will bring a sword upon you, that shall execute the
vengeance of the covenant; and ye shall be gathered together within
your cities; and I will send the pestilence among you; and ye shall
be delivered into the hand of the enemy.

26:26 When I break your staff of bread, ten women shall bake your bread in one oven, and they shall deliver your bread again by weight; and ye shall eat, and not be satisfied.
26:27 And if ye will not for all this hearken unto Me, but walk contrary unto Me;
26:28 then I will walk contrary unto you in fury; and I also will chastise you seven times for your sins.
26:29 And ye shall eat the flesh of your sons, and the flesh of your daughters shall ye eat.
26:30 And I will destroy your high places, and cut down your sun-pillars, and cast your carcasses upon the carcasses of your idols; and My soul shall abhor you.
26:31 And I will make your cities a waste, and will bring your sanctuaries unto desolation, and I will not smell the savour of your sweet odours.
26:32 And I will bring the land into desolation; and your enemies that dwell therein shall be astonished at it.
26:33 And you will I scatter among the nations, and I will draw out the sword after you; and your land shall be a desolation, and your cities shall be a waste.

The cruelty attributed to God in this passage could not be paraphrased or summarized without a complete injustice to the magnitude at which these threats are waged. Are we to believe that God will not only abandon you in the face of your enemies, but have your children killed by wild beast and have their parents to eat their children's flesh? Some may insist that the latter is figurative, despite the fact that this is literally a list of threats which seem to intensify with every word. Merely the idea of wild beast attacking a child is ungodly. We cannot believe these punishments for disobedience are the words and thoughts of God, especially considering that the reward for obedience is clearly and merely land and dominion of "their enemies."

THE DAY OF ATONEMENT

In preparation for the most important Jewish holiday, Yom Kippur, God commands Aaron (pbuh) to make sacrifices to him to atone for all of the sins of the children of Israel. This sacrifice is in conjunction with another offering. This offering is of a goat. It also brings atonement for all of the sins of the children of Israel. However this sacrifice is not to the Hebrew God, but to ANOTHER GOD named AZAZEL. Yes, God acknowledges the presence of another deity which apparently aids him in his pardon of Israel's sins. And Azazel's sacrifice is to set free one goat thus it requires no blood. This is quite unlike the Hebrew God, who requires the blood of a goat, a bull and a burnt ram. There is little wonder why the Jewish Torah has Aaron (pbuh) so confused about who or what to worship (16:3-34).

THE BOOK OF NUMBERS

Every book of the Jewish Torah must be analyzed most crucially by its depiction of God. This instantaneously speaks to the validity of the claim that God is its author. Let us explore the manner in which God is presented to us in the fourth book of the Jewish Torah, Numbers.

First we find God commanding Moses (pbuh) to make a consensus of all the children of Israel, by counting the males (1:1-2). Counting the males is common practice in the Jewish Torah and it should be understood when large amounts of Israelites are cited, this is only the male family members. Therefore, if God chose to destroy 3,000 Israelites, this number should be multiplied by at least three, if we believe the man to be married with at least one child. The question of why Israelites are counted in this way may arise in the readers mind, but also why does God need a consensus at all?

Besides satisfying some curiosity of the descendant of the Israelite, the benefit of such knowledge is difficult to grasp. Listing the sheer number of Israelites for each tribe would seem to be a product of an author which is completely infatuated with them and one who wishes his readers to be, as well. This formula found in chapter 1 and 2 is again used in chapter 26:19-62. If the Hebrew Bible is the only testament of God to man, we must admit that God has an infatuation with these people, which is unprecedented and unmatched. God wishes to highlight their lineage above every people who has ever graced this earth. This is a great testament to Israelites and those who associate themselves with Israelites, but what is to stop non-Israelites from feeling inferior in God's eyes to his favorites. This favoritism boggles the mind as we read through the Jewish Torah and in this instance, the book of Numbers, and we find that God and God's elect are not particularly fond of the Israelite's behavior, but persist in ranking them above all others. What are we to make of a God who is impartial towards a certain race of people, despite their endless transgressions in the sight of his bounteous blessings?

GOD'S ANGER TOWARDS THE HEBREWS

Upon hearing the Israelites murmur against him AGAIN, God, true to form, sends down a fire to consume them, as he had done Aaron's (pbuh) sons. Yet Moses (pbuh) prays to God and the fire abates (11:2). Without the compassion of Moses (pbuh), God may have killed them all. Of course, this punishment from God does little to hinder the Israelites from complaining about their sustenance from God. Throughout the Jewish Torah, they are depicted as ungrateful, spoiled and rebellious people towards God. And when God sets to punish them for their ingratitude, as he is reported to have done in this very instance, he is presented as "hotheaded" and in need of counsel. Moses (pbuh), the level headed man, calms God Almighty down once again and talks sense into God.

11:10 And Moses heard the people weeping, family by family, every man at the door of his tent; and the anger of HaShem was kindled greatly; and Moses was displeased.

God is enraged by the Hebrews complaining and Moses (pbuh) sidetracks God with his own complaints, namely that the rule God gave him over the people is too great a task for him to manage (11:14). And God accommodates his prophet with help to bear the burden (11:16-17). Is this how the omniscient God handles situations? Does he not assess the situation himself and resolve it, or does he need suggestions? He is capable of independently governing the entire universe, but he is incapable of solving the problems of a small group of people, without a helping hand? This theme is again presented in chapter 14. The Israelites murmured against God and almost stone some innocent men to death for criticizing them. Fortunately God comes to the innocent men's rescue. Unfortunately, Moses (pbuh) comes to God's rescue.

14:10 But all the congregation bade stone them with stones, when the glory of HaShem appeared in the tent of meeting unto all the children of Israel.
14:11 And HaShem said unto Moses: 'How long will this people despise Me? and how long will they not believe in Me, for all the signs which I have wrought among them?
14:12 I will smite them with the pestilence, and destroy them, and will make of thee a nation greater and mightier than they.'

In response to this, Moses (pbuh) suggests that God is acting out of his character. He says God is "slow to anger" (which may be hard to substantiate from the accounts of the Jewish Torah) and he is kind and forgiving of sins, yet he does punish the GUILTY. However Moses (pbuh) contradicts this notion with his next words:

14:18 visiting the iniquity of the fathers upon the children, upon the third and upon the fourth generation.

The children of the sinner is not guilty at all, thus a punishment placed upon them would be contrary to the nature of someone who is kind, forgiving and just. Then Moses (pbuh) concludes with an offer for God to pardon the Israelites. And what does God say to this?

14:20 And HaShem said: 'I have pardoned according to thy word'

God only pardoned them because of Moses' (pbuh) words and will, not his own. Then God is presented as one complaining to his messenger.

14:22 surely all those men that have seen My glory, and My signs, which I wrought in Egypt and in the wilderness, yet have put Me to proof these ten times, and have not hearkened to My voice

14:27 'How long shall I bear with this evil congregation, that keep murmuring against Me?

God's knowledge and wisdom is marginalized to such a degree in the Jewish Torah that I have heard Rabbis discussing the idea of modern Israelites disagreeing with God's decisions as prophets of old had done. How is this even a possibility? The only question should be, "Did God actually say such and such?" Once it is established that you believe he did, it is nonsensical to question its validity or merit. To believe in a fallible God is incomprehensive in my opinion. As a facilitator of a moral code, and one who judges and punishes according to this code, God's authority is immediately weakened if he is capable of violating his own rules. This violation would have been the inevitable result of God's anger had he not been calmed down by his appointed messengers. The fact that he changed his mind in such instances indicates the presence of wrongdoing. If this is the case, then who is designated to judge in his trial? Perhaps his counselor and level-headed prophet, Moses (pbuh). But what are the results when the Israelites spark the anger of both Moses (pbuh) and God?

MOSES' (pbuh) AND GOD'S ANGER TOWARDS THE HEBREWS

In chapter 16, we read that 250 elected men of the Hebrew congregation headed by a man named Korah began to question Moses' (pbuh) and Aaron's authority. Korah suggests that he and the congregation have a greater position under Godthan Moses and Aaron (pbut). In responses, Moses (pbuh) asks Korah to make an offering to God and God will chose between Moses' (pbuh) and Korah's congregation. An angered Moses (pbuh) tells God "do not respect their offering" (16:15). Along with this, we read that God asks Moses and Aaron (pbut) to separate from Korah's congregation, "that I may consume them in a moment" (16:21). I wonder if Korah knew that his test of God's support would result in fatality. Religious debates are present all over the world. Are we to surmise that the person who dies first was the loser of the debate? Nonetheless, God even devised a "new" (16:30) punishment just for those who were wrong about Moses' (pbuh) authority.

16:32 And the earth opened her mouth and swallowed them up, and their households, and all the men that appertained unto Korah, and all their goods.

Is this not enough punishment from God? Not at all. God sent a plague that killed 14,700 people (17:9-14). Without Moses (pbuh) to kindle God's fire, God's wrath is boundless.

GOD'S ANGER TOWARDS AARON AND MOSES (pbut)

Amidst all the rage and vengeance of God, do the Israelites cease in kindling his anger? Not in the least. Again they murmur against God about their lack of sustenance in the wilderness, despite the fact that God has proven himself a provider on every occasion. And he provides again as Moses (pbuh) uses his rod to cause water to spring from the rocks (20:11). Moses (pbuh) is at his breaking point. He refers to his people as "rebels" as he gathers them together. But God is so incensed that he blames the

Israelites lack of faith, on Moses' and Aaron's (pbut) lack of faith. Though Aaron (pbuh) did make the golden calf, much time had passed and it seemed that he came back in God's good graces. Moses (pbuh) when in difficulty turned to God for direction, though we read that he is said to have given God direction on occasion, as well. The accusation that they lacked faith seems unfounded. Whatever the case, God punishes Moses and Aaron (pbut), with the declaration that they will not get to the Promised Land with the Israelites. The two men dedicated to liberating the Israelites are forbidden their reward because they failed to convince a people, hell-bent on being rebellious to God, that he was real.

20:12 And HaShem said unto Moses and Aaron: 'Because ye believed not in Me, to sanctify Me in the eyes of the children of Israel, therefore ye shall not bring this assembly into the land which I have given them.'

We see here that Moses and Aaron (pbut) are both addressed and given a punishment. But just 12 verses later, we notice that the entire focus is placed on Aaron's (pbuh) shoulders.

20:24 'Aaron shall be gathered unto his people; for he shall not enter into the land which I have given unto the children of Israel, because ye rebelled against My word at the waters of Meribah.

Now Aaron (pbuh) is said to have rebelled against God. Yet Aaron's (pbuh) penalty seems to be the same, in that he will not see the Promised Land, but is it? When God says he will not see the Promised Land, he means he will not see much else either. This rather strange sequence of events concludes with Moses and Aaron's (pbut) son, leading Aaron (pbuh) to his imminent demise at the hands of God on top of a mountain (20:24-29).

This is another example of the ineptitude of the men of God in the Jewish Torah. Their sins are not merely shortcomings but they are so profound that they even warrant death from God.

BALAAM

A king by the name of Balak, son of Zippor, who had just witnessed the conquest of the Amorites by the Israelites, became afraid that his land was the next to be invaded. Balak thought that Israelites were so many that they covered the entire earth. So he summoned a certain Balaam to stop their aggression by pronouncing a curse on the Israelites. As noted in previous books of the Jewish Torah, curses are believed to work in those times. But God comes to Balaam and commands him not to curse the Israelites, because "they are blessed." God maintains an affinity for this rebellious people, but I would hope that God's command for Balaam not to curse the Israelites was for Balaam's benefit only and not for the Israelites. Otherwise, God would have been validating the belief that curses can give formidable resistance to someone or something that God has blessed. Whatever the case, Balaam tells the princes summoning him that he can't go with them to curse the people for God has command him not to.

22:12 And G-d said unto Balaam: 'Thou shalt not go with them'

We are told that later in the night, God came to Balaam and told him TO GO with the princes, but only to speak the words which God commands him to speak. However, according to the story God becomes angry with him for GOING with the princes.

22:20 And G-d came unto Balaam at night, and said unto him: 'If the men are come to call thee, rise up, go with them; but only the word which I speak unto thee, that shalt thou do.'
22:21 And Balaam rose up in the morning, and saddled his ass, and went with the princes of Moab.
22:22 And G-d's anger was kindled because he went

Is God confused? Will he command you to do a certain thing and punish you for doing what he tells you to do? The answer is God is not confused? We read a little later that an angel stops Balaam and reiterates that he is to go with the princes, "but only the word that I shall speak unto thee, that thou shalt speak.' So Balaam went with the Princes of Balak." The author of the book of Numbers made a simple mistake. He said that God was angry because Balaam "went," but it appears that the infraction was that Balaam was not going to say or had not said only the words of God. I called this a simple mistake, but it is not very simple if we regard this discrepancy as coming from God. But God would not make such a mistake. Mistakes are a signature of man.

GOD'S ANGER PROBLEM

In the story of Balaam we learn that "G-d is not a man, that He should lie; neither the son of man, that He should repent" (23:19). Yet this is contrary to the Jewish Torah's depiction of Him. As noted earlier, God is said to have repented or regretted his actions in the Jewish Torah. He regretted making mankind and he sought to wipe them off the face of the earth. Apparently God is now aware of his anger problem because in chapter 25 of Numbers, God sets measures that will ensure that he is not overly cruel to the Israelites. Unfortunately, the Israelites seem to be the sole benefactors of this mercy, though they make every effort to remain unworthy of it. Though sexual immorality is presented as a reason for God to relinquish the land of the Canaanites to Israel, it is stated that the Israelites are guilty of this same offense, along with many others. They committed "harlotry" with the daughters of Moab, as well as making sacrifices and bowing down to their gods.

Of course, God is again furious with "his people." Yet his favoritism supersedes his anger and he calls for the hanging of the chiefs, so his anger will kindle against the actual culprits (25:4). But Moses (pbuh) goes a step further and says that they must kill every man that worshipped the foreign God. The roles have changed and Moses (pbuh) now calls for blood instead of mercy, but of course he is only following the laws which prescribe death to apostates.

During this massacre, an Israelite man brought a Midianite woman to Moses (pbuh) in "the sight of all the congregation." And Aaron's (pbuh) grandson, Phinehas, took a spear and stabbed both the man and woman through the stomach and killed them. It is assumed that the man and woman were romantically involved and Phinehas actions stopped a "plague" against the children of Israel. Whether this is a plague from God or the word "plague" is used to describe the slaying of the men is unclear. But what is clear is that 24,000 Israelites died at the hands of this plague and that countless others would have died had not Phinehas killed that man and woman. God is presented as being grateful that Phinehas extinguished the fire of his own anger.

25:10 And HaShem spoke unto Moses, saying:
25:11 'Phinehas, the son of Eleazar, the son of Aaron the priest, hath turned My wrath away from the children of Israel, in that he was very jealous for My sake among them, so that I consumed not the children of Israel in My jealousy.

God seems to be in anguish about punishing Israelites, but he is matter of fact when he tells Moses (pbuh) to "harass the Midianites and smite them" (25:17). God wants them punished, not for sexual immorality but because they "beguiled" the Israelites into worshipping their gods.

MIDIANITES

Midianites were to be punished for seeking to convert their Israelite cousins to their beliefs. Apparently, the Midianites felt propagation was a tenant of their faith. Yet the Israelites did not choose to enlighten their kindred, but slaughter them instead at the supposed behest of Moses (pbuh) and God Almighty. Remember that the Israelites were not angered by the conversions, but God was and they were but his soldiers sent "to execute HaShem's vengeance on Midian" (31:3). This would mean that in the sight of God, apostasy is punishable by death and those who seek to convert Hebrews are to be killed.

Moses (pbuh) assembled 1,000 men from each tribe, making it a 12,000 man army, to fight the evangelical Midianites. So they fought the Midianites and killed every male, including their kings and even Balaam, whom God had spoken with. Yet they took their women and children as captives. They took the Midianites flock and cattle and burned their city to the ground (31:9-10). Is this how godly people act in war? Is this behavior condoned by God? Why must God avenge conversion with death and captivity? Equally amazing is the behavior of the prophet of God. When the captives are brought before Moses (pbuh), he wants to know why the Israelites have kept the women alive (31:15). It is apparent and appalling why they kept the women, but it is also appalling that Moses (pbuh) would rather have them killed than set free. Moses (pbuh) goes even further in his treacherous mind and exacts punishment upon those whom he believes to have perverted the Israelites.

31:17 Now therefore kill every male among the little ones, and kill every woman that hath known man by lying with him.
31:18 But all the women children, that have not known man by lying with him, keep alive for yourselves.

This is another defining moment in the Jewish Torah for those who believe these to be inspired words of God or even words of a man of God. If ever there was evidence that these words are inspired by someone other than God, this is it. There is no way in the world that any child should come into contact with these words of the Hebrew Scripture. In my mind, there is no reasonable or rational explanation for the words supposedly uttered by Moses (pbuh). If these are the words of God, then today in war, we are ideally to kill every man, disregarding flags of surrender, kill every male teen, toddler or baby, kill every non-virgin and keep the virgin-girls for our own selves. Can someone tell me how the Israelites determined whether or not a woman was a virgin? It is blasphemous in itself to suggest that God is the author of this message.

However the story is not over yet. The Israelites determined which "women children" were virgins. There were 32,000 virgins in all (31:35). They were counted as booty and divided amongst the Israelites, like something less than human. Just consider their feelings at the time. Imagine the multitudes killed because of obvious presumptions of previous relations. Even more defiling is that supposedly God also gets his share of the women captives. He was given 32 women (31:40). If careful consideration of this event doesn't cast doubt of the authenticity of the book as from God, then perhaps nothing else will.

Of course right after this, his chosen people provoked him again. God swore that save a select few, none of the Israelite men from 20 years old and up would see the Promised Land. He made them wander throughout the wilderness for 40 years until all of the generation "that had done evil in the sight of HaShem, was consumed." God stipulated that the condition of the promise being fulfilled was that they keep the laws, yet he does everything in his power to fulfill the promised to this "brood of sinful men" (32:14).

LAWS OF THE SABBATH

Chapter 15 describes a man gathering sticks. Perhaps it was firewood for his family's warmth, but it happens to be on the Sabbath day and there is to be no work done on the Sabbath. The children of Israel brought him before Moses, Aaron (pbut), and all the congregation, but none of them knew what to do to this man, "because it had not been declared what should be done to him." Did the author of Numbers not remember that Moses had already assembled the entire congregation together and told him that the punishment for working on the Sabbath is death?

Moses (pbuh) specifically stated that they were not to even kindle a fire in their homes (Ex. 35:2). Perhaps the author of Numbers and the author of Exodus were not the same person or maybe someone made a mistake. Whichever is true, God comes with the answer.

15:35 And HaShem said unto Moses: 'The man shall surely be put to death; all the congregation shall stone him with stones without the camp.'
15:36 And all the congregation brought him without the camp, and stoned him with stones, and he died, as HaShem commanded Moses.

Could this be a law that could be utilized today? God prescribes death for trying to keep your family warm on any Saturday?

LAWS AND WOMEN

Within the laws of the book of Numbers, we notice that women do not receive inheritance from a deceased parent under normal conditions. If a man dies, he must leave his inheritance to his son. If he has no sons, THEN the daughter is given his inheritance (27:8). We also find that a woman's oath, even an oath given to God, can be vetoed by her father or by her husband if they have "disallowed her" (30:4-9). These issues, along with the treatment of captive women of war by Moses (pbuh) and not counting them as people (1:2), present God as devaluing women. They are most often identified by their shortcomings.

MORALS

While reading through the Jewish Torah one may asked, are these people, presented as those chosen by God, good role models? Are we to follow their example? Aaron (pbuh) is described by God as disobedient (20:24), he made a golden calf, and he was a racist. He and his sister, Miriam, mocked Moses (pbuh) for marrying a Cushite woman. Though Aaron (pbuh) was not punished, his sister Miriam was stricken by God with leprous. Of course, Moses (pbuh) asks his God to cure her (12:13), yet he is unbelievably silent as he and Aaron's (pbuh) son walk Aaron (pbuh) to his death. We must remember that Moses was guilty of a lack of faith just as Aaron (pbut) was. This is in conjunction with a graven image of a serpent that God orders Moses (pbuh) to make.

In yet another instance in which the Israelites angered God, God sends serpents to bite and kill them. However they repented (21:5-7).

21:8 And HaShem said unto Moses: 'Make thee a fiery serpent, and set it upon a pole; and it shall come to pass, that every one that is bitten, when he seeth it, shall live.'
21:9 And Moses made a serpent of brass, and set it upon the pole; and it came to pass, that if a serpent had bitten any man, when he looked unto the serpent of brass, he lived.

This would seem rather reckless to do when we realize how easily the Israelites can be swayed away for the true God. It seems unlikely that this jealous and underappreciated God would give them the opportunity to believe someone or something other than he had cured their bite. But back to the point, Moses (pbuh) making a graven image is not something which should be followed. And most importantly, Moses' (pbuh) lost of sanity after the fight against the Midianites is not to set any type of standard worth following. All these things lead to the reader pondering the morality, ethics and justice of God.

Does he endorse this kind of behavior? Does God give permission to sack lands, even if the inhabitants are merely defending themselves from slaughter? Because they are a chosen people will "HaShem hearkened to the voice of Israel, and delivered up the Canaanites; and they utterly destroyed them and their cities" (21:13). If you refused to allow a people to pass through your borders, will God grant them permission to kill you and steal all of your land and cities (21:23-25)? If these chosen people dwell in this land but are unsatisfied with it and decide to conquer another land, is it morally right to smite the king, "and his sons, and all his people, until there was none left him remaining; and they possessed his land" (21:35)? To sidestep this issue of morality, those who believe this to be the words of God might argue that it is God who apparently deemed it morally right for Israel to conquer these territories given their success rate in the Jewish Torah. If success in conquest is means by which we determine whose side God is on, we might wonder about all the great, yet despicable conquerors of history.

As we read the Jewish Torah, it becomes abundantly clear that God is obsessed with the heritage of the Israelite people and with the conquest of land already inhabited, especially the land of the Canaanites (33:50-56, 34:1-2). This obsession leads me to believe that the author is not God, but an Israelite who is intent on instilling Israelite nationalism in the people. Yet its immediate effect could lead to the kind of racism Aaron (pbuh) and Miriam displayed.

Does God condone these battles of conquest? They are called "The Wars of HaShem" and they are mentioned as being noted in a mysterious book (21:14). The brutality described in the Jewish Torah is enough to make a case against the idea that God condoned such wars, but the idea that there exists an even more detailed account of these acts warps the mind. What could the book possibly contain? Vivid descriptions of killings of all the males and explaining the captivity of the females? God's name should be far from this kind of a book.

DEUTERONOMY

Now we come to the last of the books of the Jewish Torah. What do you think might be the topic? What might be the last and most resounding message left by "Moses" to the Israelites? Well it is the same message that permeates the entire Jewish Torah, follow the laws of God and God will give you land. It is believed by Bible scholars that Deuteronomy has an author independent from the other books of the Jewish Torah, though they do not believe this author to be Moses (pbuh). This book does seem to cover the laws all in a nutshell.

"OUR GOD"

The author is a strategic propagandist. Though the other books of the Jewish Torah mention that the Israelites are God's chosen people and they make mention that God is described as "their" God, this sentiment is multiplied 20 times over in Deuteronomy. God is mentioned as "our God" and as "your God" such a ridiculous amount of times (over 300 times in one book) that it has to be purposeful. As a non-Jew reading this, I can't help but feel inferior if I believe these words to be truly inspired by God. As a Jew, this kind of statement is intended to build your self-esteem and morale, but it ultimately leads to a superiority complex. In spite of all their transgressions, God is still "theirs." This gives the insinuation that God is only "their" God. Deuteronomy cited several instances in which God is angry at the Israelites or he is angry at Moses because of the Israelites (1:35, 37, 3:26, 4:21, 11:17). Despite his constant displeasure with them, God declared

7:6 ... thou art a holy people unto HaShem thy G-d: HaShem thy G-d hath chosen thee to be His own treasure, out of all peoples that are upon the face of the earth.
7:7 HaShem did not set His love upon you, nor choose you, because ye were more in number than any people--for ye were the fewest of all peoples-
7:8 but because HaShem loved you, and because He would keep the oath which He swore unto your fathers, hath HaShem brought you out with a mighty hand, and redeemed you out of the house of bondage, from the hand of Pharaoh king of Egypt.

Amazingly, in Deuteronomy, God is said to show no favoritism (10:17), yet he loves these people above everyone else not for any act of righteousness or belief, but because he made a promise to their forefathers, Abraham, Isaac and Jacob (pbut). This is almost an unconditional love, because it's based on a promised. The only condition God places on the Israelites is to keep the laws and commandments and they will keep the Promised Land (5:28, 11:1, 12:28, 13:1). God delivers their enemies to them, so the Israelites can smite them and destroy them, forming no treaties with them, nor showing any mercy (7:2). The Hebrew Scriptures characterize the inhabitants of the land as "enemies" of Israel (32:27, 42, 33:27). If you call someone your enemy, whether they are or they are not, most assuredly they will become your enemy, eventually.

Non-Israelites are ignored or at the very best, a distant afterthought. In Deuteronomy, Israelite's seizure of others' land and killing of the people is credited to God (2:12, 21-25) Throughout the Jewish Torah and throughout the Hebrew Scriptures as a whole, God sends prophet after prophet to "his" people. If you believe this is the sole source of truth from God, then God left out the bulk of humanity. How can Israelites not feel superior to those people? This superiority complex, and its endorsement as from God, gave the Israelites the courage and temerity to go land to land killing people, destroying their buildings, capturing their women and daughters and removing any traces of the people who had not harmed them in the least.

One may ask, how can some people kill another human being without remorse? The answer is brainwashing. If you tell people over and over that God said you can do this, it becomes reasonable to them and they can carry out the most horrible deeds without remorse. Every person is susceptible to this conditioning, no matter your race, religion or education. The reason this condition has not been diagnosed is because most people believe it's true. They believe the Jewish Torah to be the words of God. Everyday there are reports of Muslims who believe it is God's orders to kill some innocent people. Those who believe in the Bible are at times the most vocal critics of these Muslims. There are some who even indict the religion of Islam for these Muslims views, yet they are not mindful of the annihilation of the innocent families that God has ordered in their own scriptures.

HENOTHEISM

As first mentioned in Exodus, God is a jealous god (4:24, 5:9), but who is he jealous of? Judaism is a monotheistic religion, but was the early Israelites henotheist? The belief in monotheism seems to be what is discussed in chapter 4.

4:35 Unto thee it was shown, that thou mightiest know that HaShem, He is G-d; there is none else beside Him.

At face value, this seems to give strong indication of a belief in one God. It even seems to deny the existence of any other gods. But if it is read in its proper context, it seems to fit henotheism perfectly.

4:36 Out of heaven He made thee to hear His voice, that He might instruct thee; and upon earth He made thee to see His great fire; and thou didst hear His words out of the midst of the fire.
4:37 And because He loved thy fathers, and chose their seed after them, and brought thee out with His presence, with His great power, out of Egypt,
4:38 to drive out nations from before thee greater and mightier than thou, to bring thee in, to give thee their land for an inheritance, as it is this day;
4:39 know this day, and lay it to thy heart, that HaShem, He is G-d in heaven above and upon the earth beneath; there is none else.

This declaration by God is to the Israelites only. As shown earlier, the God is "their" God. He made them specifically to hear his voice and rule over the other nations. So when it says there is no other God, it means no other God for the Israelites. This must be the case. Otherwise, the mentioning of "other" gods in the Jewish Torah is unexplained. They are not called false gods, but "other," "foreign" or "alien" gods meaning other than the God of Abraham, Isaac and Jacob (pbut). Deuteronomy continuously mentions other gods (7:4, 11:28, 13:7, 17:3, 29:26, 31:18, 20) and it mentions foreign gods of other lands (31:16). And 10:17 seems to seal the deal on henotheism of the Israelites.

10:17 For HaShem your G-d, He is G-d of gods, and L-rd of lords, the great G-d, the mighty, and the awful.

THE NATURE OF GOD

The God of the Israelites does not shun advice from his creation. In chapter 9 and 10, Moses (pbuh) is said to have offered God numerous suggestions and God hearkens to his advice every time. This God detests certain pillars that the Israelites might build (16:22). Is there good enough reason for God to actually hate or detest something so minuscule? If the Hebrews do not follow the laws, God will not forgive them and his anger and jealous will be kindled (29:19). Also this God will be happy "to cause you to perish and to destroy you and ye shall be plucked from off the land whither thou goest in to possess it" (28:63). God knows full well what the consequences of these actions will be. He says the Israelites will be scatter all over the earth and they will fall prey to the worship of other gods. So why would he rejoice? Their worship of other gods will only lead to more jealousy, more anger and more wrath from God. Then they will become worthless or dispensable to God as were the Amorites, Canaanites, Midianites etc.

ISRAELITES

Deuteronomy basically summarizes the Israelites experiences. Throughout the book, the message is "your" God is giving you the land of the Canaanites, and if you obey his laws, you will remain in the land forever. Of course, they couldn't get to the land without upsetting God and Moses (pbuh) of multiple occasions. The anger of God is duly noted. But Moses (pbuh) had a few chose words for his people, as well. Moses (pbuh) rebukes them for their transgressions from the first chapter onwards (1:43) and calls them "stiff-necked" (31:27). Moses (pbuh) says "Ye have been rebellious against HaShem from the day that I knew you (9:24)," yet he pleads with God not to destroy them, and "look not unto the stubbornness of this people, nor to their wickedness, nor to their sin" (9:27).

However, we read that the wickedness of the inhabitants of the Promised Land is the reason that the land is being given to the Israelites. How does this make sense, when we read that the Israelites are wicked as well? The

Canaanites and others are accused of burning their own children, and of consorting with soothsayers and sorcerers. Yet the Israelites killed scores of men, women and male children and they keep the virgins for themselves. They also fell victim to worshipping gods other than the God of Abraham (pbuh). So they have little moral ground to stand upon. Yet, God is intent on setting these people "high over all nations" (28:1) and they will be made to "rule over other nations, but other nations are not to rule over them." They are allowed to lend but not to borrow from other nations (15:4-6).

Does God choose these people above all others on earth because they are the best of the worse? It would appear that God overlooks their misdeeds in order to fulfill a promise that he made. And this Promised Land is to be obtained when "HaShem drives out all these nations" (11:23). There is constant reference to the fear of Israel put into the inhabitants of the land, but there is not a single word of redemption for these people.

There is also the absence of the God of Israel to include anyone other than Israel into his fold. There exists no inclination to extend a helping hand to the inhabitants, no inclination on God's part to overlook the misdeeds of non-Israelites, or to grant them some newfound enlightenment. This God seems to be uninterested in conversion. Of the 613 commandments, there is not one which suggests that Israelites should reach out to others for their conversion, despite the existence of several rules that a "stranger" or "foreigner" must follow when they are amongst the Israelites. This begs the question, how are the Canaanites violators of God's moral code when they are unaware that it exists? Even if God were to instruct the Israelites to proselytize their beliefs, it would fall on death ears, since the Israelites foreign policy was to kill the males and women and take their land and take their virgins. Who would sincerely consider the beliefs of an evangelist whose alternative to his faith is theft and murder?

LAWS

Did you know that crucifixion is a permissible punishment in the Hebrew Scriptures? I am sure those who practice Judaism know this, but I wonder if this fact registers in the mind of a Christian. I would imagine that their love for Jesus (pbuh) and his supposed self-sacrifice obscures the fact that the penalty that he is believed to have endured may be used today (see my book "Jesus Was Not Crucified"). And its practice is Biblically approved (21:22-23). In fact, as one who adhered to the law, he would have condoned crucifixion himself for those deserving this punishment. But this is just one punishment in Deuteronomy.

As in the previous books, there are laws throughout the book of Deuteronomy as well as the punishment for violating these laws. For instances, if a prophet tells the Israelites to worship "other gods," he is to be put to death (13:2-6). Not only a prophet, but if your friend, your wife, your brother or your own child were to suggest to you the worship of other gods, they are to be stoned to death, publicly and you are to be the first to cast the stones (13:711). If the suggestion of apostasy is grounds for death, then the actual act must carry the same punishment. In the very same chapter we read that Israelites are commanded to investigate the convictions of their brothers diligently, and if it is found that they have submitted to another God, they are to be destroyed utterly (13:13-16).

Deuteronomy is in full agreement with the laws of the rest of the Jewish Torah, that apostasy is punishable by death. For further explanation of this matter, we find in chapter 17 that two or three witnesses must testify to the apostasy of this man or woman, 1 witness is not sufficient for capital punishment. The witnesses are to cast the first stones, and then the community must follow. If there is a case in which an Israelite worships other gods, yet the case is too hard to judge, the judge must get his verdict from the Levite priests. If he doesn't heed the verdict prescribed by the priest, then he is to be put to death (17:12). God is said to command that in killing a person, even if it's your own child, you are to show no pity (13:9, 19:3, 19:21). Is this the God in which we believe to be merciful, just and forgiving? God's nature is confusing in the Jewish Torah, for example:

20:10 When thou drawest nigh unto a city to fight against it, then proclaim peace unto it.

Do you see the contradiction in this verse? The Israelites are going to fight against a certain people, yet they say they are there in peace. There was a very bad movie entitled "I Come in Peace" in which an alien would say these very words and then kill everyone he encountered. When I read this verse, I get the impression that this is a false peace to lure the enemy into submission without battle. And the next verse confirms my suspicions, because the Israelites are commanded by "God" to enslave those who accept their peace offering.

20:11 And it shall be, if it make thee answer of peace, and open unto thee, then it shall be, that all the people that are found therein shall become tributary unto thee, and shall serve thee.

So what is the alternative to peace and slavery?

20:12 And if it will make no peace with thee, but will make war against thee, then thou shalt besiege it.

20:13 And when HaShem thy G-d delivereth it into thy hand, thou shalt smite every male thereof with the edge of the sword;

20:14 but the women, and the little ones, and the cattle, and all that is in the city, even all the spoil thereof, shalt thou take for a prey unto thyself; and thou shalt eat the spoil of thine enemies, which HaShem thy G-d hath given thee.

Again we see the harsh manner in which God is supposed to instruct Israelites to deal with others. More alarming is the idea that God will aid in this evil against men, women and "the little ones." God gets more specific as he pronounces the utter destruction of "the Hittite, and the Amorite, the Canaanite, and the Perizzite, the Hivite, and the Jebusite" because of their sins (20:1718), while he remains forgetful about the multitude of transgressions perpetuated by "his people." He also commands that the Israelites "shalt save alive nothing that breatheth" (20:16). What is the purpose of such barbarism?

One might wonder what to do with a rebellious and stubborn son. Well the Jewish Torah says if he is rebellious and stubborn and he is a gluttonous, drunkard, his parents are to have him stoned to death (21:18-21). This may be harsh and unfair, but there are laws which attempt to keep stability in the home, like countering the favoritism of parents for one child over and another.

In the case of a man with two wives, one in which he loves and another in which he hates, if the hated wife is the mother of the man's firstborn son, that son is to get his firstborn rights and double the portion of the son of the beloved wife. This seems to be a just law in the spirit that the child is not penalized or rewarded based upon the current relationship of the parents. This is despite the unfairness of a firstborn getting more than his siblings. But the problem I have with this law is that it is waved on numerous occasions in the Jewish Torah, in order to give preference to the Israelites (i.e. Ishmael and Isaac, Esau and Jacob). Thus this law is to combat the favoritism of the parents, yet God evokes his own favoritism with no moral or ethically ground to stand on.

In chapter 14, we read the permissible and prohibited food given in the laws. Some of the permissible animals to eat are the clean bird, the goat and the sheep. Prohibited meat includes that of a pig, a camel or a hare. The law also forbids the eating of an animal that died of natural causes. The Hebrews are not to eat of this meat, but strangely enough God permits them to give this meat to strangers or sell it to foreigners (14:21). Apparently, God is more interested in the Israelites' health, whereas the rest of the world's health is of little importance. Speaking of interest, it is prohibited for Israelites to charge interest to another Israelite. However it is permissible for him to charge interest to a foreigner (23:20-21)? Such double standards cannot be attributed to God.

WOMEN

There are several laws which deal with women and how they are to live their lives. Just as homosexuality is described as an abomination in the Jewish Torah, a woman wearing men's clothing is also an abomination before God (22:5). If a husband is suspicious of his wife's virginity, the woman's father and mother must provide proof of her virginity in the presence of the elders of the city (22:13-22). Proof of virginity? Whatever the method used, it was undoubtedly flawed, however the penalty is still administered. If the man is found to be wrong, he is to pay 100 shekels of silver to the FATHER, and he is to remain married to this woman, FOREVER. He can never divorce her. But if the husband's charges are found to be correct.

22:21 then they shall bring out the damsel to the door of her father's house, and the men of her city shall stone her with stones that she dies

The poor woman loses in both scenarios. If the case is baseless, she still suffers humiliation from the public and her parents suffer the same humiliation, but her father gets 100 shekels for defamation of "his" character. And she wins an eternity with her untrusting husband. And if it is found that she was not a virgin at the time of her marriage, she is to be stoned to death on her FATHER'S doorstep. The fact that the father is mentioned in the punishment is an attempt to cast blame and humiliation at his feet, as well. We are then told that the punishment for adultery is death (22:22). But what about a woman who is engaged to a man and she is found with another man? They too are to be put to death.

Chapter 22 ends with an even more disturbing scenario in which a virgin damsel is neither married nor engaged. If a man "lay hold on her, and lies with her," he is to give her father 50 shekels of silver. And he is to marry his victim and never divorce her (22:28-29). Again the father's image is placed at the forefront, while the victim is to live in matrimony with this rapist forever. Can we ascribe this kind of thinking to God?

Other laws involved men who die childless. If this case arises, the woman is not to married "abroad" (25:5), but she must marry the deceased's brother and their firstborn son is to be accredited to the deceased. As I have stated earlier these laws were in effect long before Moses (pbuh) received them because the story found in Genesis about brothers, Er and Onan, indicate the very essence of this law. The unfairness Onan perceived, because the seed would not be his, is overshadowed by the denial of the widow to marry someone other than her former husband's brother. God kills Onan for not following this commandment. Adding insult to injury (actually death), we are told that the widow in this case is allowed to "spit in the face" of the brother who refused to heed this commandment (25:9-10). Is there possibly a rationale for God to propose such behavior?

The last law dealing with women which I find to be incompatible with the nature of a just and fair God is the case which involves two men fighting or grappling. If the wife of one of the men intervenes in order to help her husband and she grabs his opponent's private parts, her hand is to be severed, WITHOUT PITY (25:11-12).

To say that this punishment is to be administered without pity indicates that it may be immoral in the eyes of the general public. In desperation, a woman hits a man where it hurts to free her hapless husband. Should this action even be litigated at all, provided that she did not go to any extremes after freeing her husband? Would God concern himself with such a situation? Perhaps this law is in contrast to my own opinion, but I find it to be a law in which a man might invent.

OTHER LAWS

The laws of the Jewish Torah contain other restrictions pertaining to a man's private part in which I find ungodly. Those men who have been injured or deformed in this area are not to enter the congregation of God (23:2). Likewise children born out of wedlock are turned away by the congregation of God (23:3).

Apparently the author assumes that God thinks unfavorably of the afflicted and the offspring of fornication, when in no way are they guilty of any offense. Perhaps because they are born in this manner, the superstitious author believes God has cursed them and this curse may besiege the congregation. Degradation, humiliation and ostracizing are all punishments and punishment denotes that a crime or sin has been committed by the person bearing the burden, but of course this is not the case at all. These afflictions are seen as punishments for the parents of the victim for whatever wrongdoing they had done. And the child out of wedlock is deemed a curse as well.

The child's ostracism punishes the parent and the child. The person suffering the deformity is never to enter the congregation and the "bastard" (as the word is translated in English) can't enter the congregation of 10 generations. This means their children's children's children's children's children are still accursed and punished for the actions of two people, not 10 years but 10 GENERATIONS. There are vast differences of opinions on the length of time a generation is, especially in Biblical terms. They range from 25 years to 100 years and possibly beyond that. Let us assume the lowest at 25 years. This would mean that the actions of the two people who fornicated were punished for at least 250 more years. Whatever the case, 10 generations of sons, daughters and their children are punished by God simply because they were born. The Ammonite and Moabite children are punished in like manner.

23:4 An Ammonite or a Moabite shall not enter into the assembly of HaShem; even to the tenth generation shall none of them enter into the assembly of HaShem for ever

We must remember the Moabites and Ammonites are the descendants of Lot and this punishment is in response to the Moabites refusing to give the Israelites food and water and their hiring of Balaam to curse the Israelites. The Ammonites are not mentioned at all in Numbers 22, but the author lumps them all together in this condemnation. Disregarding the fact that the Israelites were conquering and killing everyone in their path, these people's refusal to oblige the Israelites and their seeking of aid in fighting against them are not grounds to punish their children for 10 generations (or forever). This idea of punishing the child for the acts of the father goes against all fairness and justice. In fact it goes against the Jewish Torah's own teachings.

24:16 The fathers shall not be put to death for the children, neither shall the children be put to death for the fathers; every man shall be put to death for his own sin.

Is this not the more just and fair approach to crime and punishment? Would we not frown upon a judicial system which penalizes the child for the sins of their parents? So, how can we entertain the notion that God governs in such an unjust manner?

MOSES (pbuh)

We now come to the central character in the Jewish Torah, Moses (pbuh). He is described throughout the Jewish Torah as a brave, determined and a by-the-book (or the law) person. He is passionate about his mission and he becomes enraged when his people disbelieve or doubt God. Yet he is not always cased in the brightest light. In Deuteronomy as in the other books, Moses (pbuh) seems at times to be unworthy of prophethood. His actions, described in the Jewish Torah, cast doubt on the ability of God to chose a worthy prophet. It is Moses (pbuh) who comes with words of peace and leaves behind none alive, not even "the little ones."

After such treachery, we find Moses (pbuh) bragging about his conquest and the death toll, spoils and land he acquired (3:6-11). Moses (pbuh), the wise advisor, changes God's mind about killing the Israelites on numerous occasions. And perhaps weary from Moses' (pbuh) constant advice, God on one occasion told Moses (pbuh)

9:14 Let me alone, that I may destroy them

This one verse speaks volumes about Moses (pbuh) and about the God of the Jewish Torah.

MY CONCLUSION

THE GOAL AND SUMMATION OF THE JEWISH TORAH

We must first realize that there is no place in the Jewish Torah which states that God wrote or inspired the words in it, aside from the Ten Commandments. We ought not to attribute to God things which he does not attribute to himself. Had he inspired these words, it seems logical that he would have indicated this. We must also admit that the author does not suggest that God inspired him. This is an assumption made by readers and conveyed to the masses. There exists quite a contrast between words in which you believe to be true and words in which you believe to be God's. The former has room for error, the latter does not. The third point to be made is that the Jewish Torah was not autographed. It is traditionally held that Moses (pbuh) wrote the Jewish Torah or that these were the inspired words of God to Moses (pbuh). However one may be hard-pressed to find any scholar of the Hebrew scripture who will give Moses (pbuh) the credit of writing the Jewish Torah.

"..there is hardly a biblical scholar in the world actively working on the [authorship] problem who would claim that the Five Books of Moses were written by Moses." R.E. Friedman.

As mentioned earlier most believe the books to be from an unknown author or numerous authors. Those who promote the idea of numerous authors suggest that Deuteronomy had its own author, whereas the other books may have had a collage of stories by different authors combined together to produce the books we read today. It seems Deuteronomy is a summation of the laws and the conquests of Moses (pbuh) and the Israelite people. Doubts of Moses (pbuh) as the Jewish Torah's author emerge when the reader realizes the books of the Jewish Torah are written in third person. Over 700 times we read that "HaShem said to Moses" and "Moses said to HaShem." The first four books are written in third person throughout. But the book of Deuteronomy contains a few quotations in the first person. The sudden use of these direct quotes from Moses (pbuh) gives some the impression that the author of this book is not the same author of the rest of the Jewish Torah. The first person usage is understood as quotations of Moses (pbuh) by a third party because the book begins with and leads throughout as a book which is "about" God and Moses (pbuh), not "by" them.

1:1 These are the words which Moses spoke unto all Israel beyond the Jordan

28:69 These are the words of the covenant which HaShem commanded Moses to make with the children of Israel in the land of Moab, beside the covenant which He made with them in Horeb.

31:1 And Moses went and spoke these words unto all Israel.
31:2 And he said unto them: 'I am a hundred and twenty years old this day; I can no more go out and come in

The notion that Moses (pbuh) wrote the Jewish Torah may come from the misunderstanding of these words, "And Moses wrote this law" (31:9). It's quite obvious that the Jewish Torah is a chronological story from the beginning of time to the rise of the Israelites. Within this story are the numerous laws which they must live by. The author of the Jewish Torah we have today was speaking of the book of laws which Moses (pbuh) wrote, not these stories. But because the Jewish Torah is perceives as the laws of Moses (pbuh), some have mistakenly attributed all of the books to Moses (pbuh), when in fact, none of these books are by Moses (pbuh). The laws contained in the Jewish Torah are from some unknown author who we are to believe accurately reproduced them. The fact that this author tells us that Moses (pbuh) wrote the laws, which were to be read at the "feast of the tabernacle" (31:1011), shows that it was not a collection of the five books of the Jewish Torah because the people at the feast were "to do all the words of this law" (31:12). The Jewish Torah has numerous stories and laws that should not and cannot be observed. It would be a great disservice to Moses (pbuh) and God to attribute the laws we have discussed to either of them. It is more likely that 1 or more authors comprised their own books filled with laws and stories they heard. And they added and subtracted what they liked to fit their agenda. This would better explain the inconsistencies and immoralities contained in these books of the Jewish Torah. I am inclined to believe the author(s) had no idea that most of the believers of this book would accredit it to Moses (pbuh). When reading the books it is clear that someone is writing about his life and experiences. Probably the nail in the coffin is in last chapter of Deuteronomy.

34:5 So Moses the servant of HaShem died there in the land of Moab, according to the word of HaShem.
34:6 And he was buried in the valley in the land of Moab over against Beth-peor; and no man knoweth of his sepulchre unto this day.
34:7 And Moses was a hundred and twenty years old when he died: his eye was not dim, nor his natural force abated.

Did Moses (pbuh) write this? So we are to believe that Moses (pbuh) not only wrote about his own birth, but about his death, as well. Would he write that he DIED and was BURIED when he was 120 years old? Had this been a revelation given to him, he would have stated that he WILL DIE and BE BURIED when he is 120 years old. Even more clear is that Deuteronomy 34:10 says there has not been a prophet like Moses (pbuh) SINCE his DEATH. Is there anymore doubt that these are not his words, but the words of someone who lived along time after Moses (pbuh)? This means the author of the Jewish Torah which we have today is in direct violation of the laws of Moses (pbuh).

4:2 Ye shall not add unto the word which I command you, neither shall ye diminish from it, that ye may keep the commandments of HaShem your G-d which I command you.

Adding stories to the law is a sin according to this. The prophet Jeremiah attests to this author's perversion of the scriptures of Moses (pbuh).

Jeremiah 8:8 "How can you say, 'We are wise, and the law of the Lord is with us'? But, behold, the false pen of the scribes has made it into a lie."

The Jews said they have the Jewish Torah, and Jeremiah says no you have the lying words of the scribes. This cannot be emphasized enough. A prophet of God testifies in a book of God that the Jewish Torah that the Jews have is not the real Torah. Jeremiah made the same argument thousands of years ago that I make today. All these things assure us that these are not the words of God. But the story does not end with the Jewish Torah.

Within in the pages of the Hebrews scripture, you will find God making his prophet walk naked for three YEARS (imagine such a thing in front of your parents, children and co-workers), God spreading dung on people's faces, God making people eat human excrement, you will find love letters describing the human anatomy, and other things far from one's idea of information found in a book of God. Throughout the pages of the Bible, there are more tales of the impotence of God, more examples of prophets performing the most heinous crimes, more acts of genocide performed by the Israelites, more unchecked sexual immorality and more authors perpetuating their overtly biased views. This cannot be the words of God or even true men of God.

WHAT THIS MEANS FOR CHRISTIANS?

As I have said early in this book, Jesus (pbuh) instructs his followers to obey and teach these laws until "heaven and earth pass away." Heaven and earth have not passed away yet, thus it is incumbent upon those who profess to be his followers to follow him. In that regard, they must admit that if their scriptures are true then Jesus (pbuh) adhered to all the laws mentioned in the Jewish Torah, and he endorsed all the penalties prescribed for disobeying these laws, aside from the very few laws which he abrogated. In order to be Christ-like, the Christian must do the same. The Christian must confess that according to his beliefs, Jesus (pbuh) supported slavery, bigotry, murder, theft of land, death for apostasy, death for practicing witchcraft, death for disrespecting your parents, death for adultery and death for homosexuality. They must accept that God is not all-wise, that he is not infallible and that he ignored the entire world for thousands of years, and focused solely on a small group of people.

The Christian religion is a shining example of what will inevitably formulate from a non-Jew who holds the Jewish Torah to be the words of God. Christians have accepted a Jewish man as God Almighty. Because of their belief in the Jewish Torah, they are effectively propagandized into believing that Jews are the chosen people and they are the primary recipients of God's prophets and his message, until finally God became a Jew and chose them. Then came another Jewish man, Paul, who created their entire religion for them. This is how they can concede that a gentile woman and her sick daughter are dogs in comparison to Jews, simply because they are non-Jews (Matt. 15:26). This is how they can view the Palestinian and Israeli conflict from a Jewish standpoint alone. It is time that the Christians read the Jewish Torah and view things objectively.

"The Jewish Bible is not God's story of Israel, but Israel's story of Israel" - Marcus Borg, "JESUS: Uncovering the Life, Teachings, and Relevance of a Religious Revolutionary"

THE GREAT OMISSION

At this point, I am comfortable that I have established the case that neither God, nor Moses (pbuh) (if you believe him to be a true prophet of God) wrote these words of the Jewish Torah. But perhaps the crowning argument is the overall theme of the Jewish Torah and the crucial details that it lacks as an inspired scripture from God. Any reader of these five books would be forced to admit that the scope of the Jewish Torah is obedience of the Israelite people in order for them to receive land, earthly and physical land. The fact that five books of the Jewish Torah are fixated on a particular promise to a particular group of people with very little to say about man's purpose on earth, the rewards and punishments given by God after life and man's final destination is the ultimate revelation that these books are not from God. The Jewish Torah is filled with chapters of names of men and their first begotten sons. God gives five books worth of instructions on how to take people's land, but he reveals absolutely nothing on how to attain an abode in Heaven.

If your primary goal in life is to live a righteous life in order to see God in Paradise, the Jewish Torah is not the book for you, if you read it at face value. But if you are equipped with certain knowledge you can read the Hebrew Scriptures and get a very different picture than what is on the surface. After reading the Qur'an and its description of Paradise for ALL those who submit to the will of God, it is abundantly clear that the land described in the Hebrew Scripture is not physical land but what some may call Heaven.

Though the Jewish Torah is deficient in its mention of the afterlife, one-third of the Qur'an is dedicated to the subject. The Qur'an does confirm that God ordained land for the Israelites. Of course, there is no mention of displacing another group of people to gain this land. There is also confirmation in the Qur'an that many of the Israelites were rebellious to God. But the author of the Jewish Torah seems to confuse and converge the physical land with the PROMISED LAND of Paradise which ALL the God-fearing and Law-adhering people will receive.

Exodus 33:2 and I will send an angel before thee; and I will drive out the Canaanite, the Amorite, and the Hittite, and the Perizzite, the Hivite, and the Jebusite-Exodus
Exodus 33:3 unto a land flowing with milk and honey

Deuteronomy 6:3 Hear, O Israel, and be careful to obey so that it may go well with you and that you may increase greatly in a land flowing with milk and honey, just as the Lord , the God of your fathers, promised you (also Deut. 26:15, 27:3)

Al-Quran 47:15 (Here is) a Parable of the Garden which the righteous are promised: in it are rivers of water incorruptible: rivers of milk of which the taste never changes; rivers of wine a joy to those who drink; and rivers of honey pure and clear. In it there are for them all kinds of fruits and Grace from their Lord.(Can those in such Bliss) be compared to such as shall dwell forever in the Fire, and be given, to drink, boiling water, so that it cuts up their bowels (to pieces)?

The author of the Jewish Torah is using the words "milk and honey" to describe a place which is serene and pleasurable. The Qur'an does the same. We know from further reading of the Hebrew Scriptures that the land which the Israelites acquired was and is to this day everything but a calm, peaceful and pleasant place to live. The Qur'anic verse above is a description of Paradise and a description of some of the pleasures the righteous will receive after death. It is a parable or allegory of the pleasures and discomforts of the life after death. In light of the numerous conflicts waged in the land of promise and assaults waged upon its inhabitants, the pleasant description would better fit the gardens of Paradise, than the land of the Canaanites.

With the mentioning of the parable of the gardens in Paradise, I am obliged to expound upon the view that Muslims are prohibited from drinking wine on earth but they are given wine in heaven. First off, the verse begins with the indication that this is a parable. A parable is a simple story illustrating a moral or religious lesson. They are very seldom, if ever, taken literally, but used for their moral value. If one was to insist that this verse is to be taken literally, there is absolutely no problem with this standpoint. ALLAH is all-knowing and he has given the Muslim an answer to those who may inquiry about this matter.

Al-Quran 76:21 Upon them will be green Garments of fine silk and heavy brocade, and they will be adorned with Bracelets of silver; and their Lord will give to them to drink of a Wine Pure and Holy.
Al-Quran 37:43 In Gardens of Felicity,
Al-Quran 37:44 Facing each other on Thrones (of Dignity):
Al-Quran 37:45 Round will be passed to them a Cup from a clear-flowing fountain,
Al-Quran 37:46 Crystal-white, of a taste delicious to those who drink (thereof),
Al-Quran 37:47 Free from headiness; nor will they suffer intoxication therefrom.

As you can see, this is not a wine which intoxicates. It is pure and holy.

JESUS (pbuh) REJECTED

Because of this great omission of the hereafter, the Holy Prophet Jesus (pbuh) was rejected by the people of Israel. They expected the Messiah to be "like Moses" and led them triumphantly from under the authority of the Romans. The Israelites, taking cue from the Jewish Torah in their possession, were chiefly concerned with worldly gain, not spiritual gain. When Jesus (pbuh) said his kingdom is not of this world, he was referring to his reward after death. He stressed that the Jews misunderstand the law and its purpose. The scripture they read convinced them that God gives them their reward, and then they must follow the laws. Jesus (pbuh) emphasized that they follow God's laws first, and then they will receive an everlasting reward. With the understanding that the Jewish Torah which is in existence today is not the words of God or his prophet, it becomes clear that this book and its constant focus of earthly possessions and its marginalized view of life after death, is a huge factor in why Jesus (pbuh) was rejected by the people. They were convinced that victory is only through land and power. Obedience to God is but a means to achieve this victory. Heaven was the furthest thing from their minds.

THE QUR'AN AND THE JEWISH TORAH

THE QUR'AN THE CORRECTION AND COMPLETION

Before delving any further into the Qur'an, let me first clarify a misconception about the Qur'an and the Jewish Torah. The Qur'an pays great tribute to the Torah. The Torah is believed to be the revelation from God given to Moses (pbuh) a great prophet of God. Obviously, Muslims do not believe the books we have today to be the revelation given to Moses (pbuh) for all the reasons mentioned in this book. The true Torah of Moses (pbuh) has not been found. This may be because it was a revelation transmitted orally and was never committed to paper. The Qur'an says God causes his revelations to be forgotten throughout time and he replaces it with something better.

Al-Qur'an 2:106 None of Our revelations do We abrogate or cause to be forgotten, but We substitute something better or similar: Knowest thou not that Allah Hath power over all things?

The circumstances surrounding the Israelites at that time called for laws which would be inapplicable in today's times. They were a nomadic people. Traveling throughout the desert for years, there is no time for lengthy trials, so their laws were probably stiff and their justice swift. A group of people who have settled in an area for a long period of time would naturally have more steps in their due process. In that light and to minimize confusion from a nomadic rule of thumb, it is advantageous to have a different set of rules to govern different societies. This is perhaps why there are a multitude of prophets. As society and circumstances change, God sends his messengers to present his will to the people as it pertains to them specifically. The Qur'an states that prophets were sent to every people (16:36). God is not fixated only on one group of people. God's chosen people are ALL those who do his will.

Al-Qur'an 47:38 Behold, ye are those invited to spend (of your substance) in the Way of Allah: But among you are some that are niggardly. But any who are niggardly are so at the expense of their own souls. But Allah is free of all wants, and it is ye that are needy. If ye turn back (from the Path), He will substitute in your stead another people; then they would not be like you!

This is quite a different response from that given in the Jewish Torah, in which God is overwhelmed with grief, jealousy and vengeance against those whom turn from the right path. The Qur'an insists that turning from the right path will harm you, not God. Acting selfishly with your blessing is another point not discussed in the Jewish Torah. It is true that God chose the Israelites, but he chose them to do his will and teach this to others. They were not chosen to rule others but to enjoin others to do God's will. In a very similar manner, God chose the Arab nation, which is the cousin of the Hebrew nation, to deliver God's message, to deliver the final call to Islam. The Qur'an was revealed to an Arab, in Arabic and it was to be delivered first to Arabs. Because God chose them, does that make them superior to anyone else? According to the Qur'an, not at all! God judges based upon action and intent, not race or ethnicity. We know that all were at one point in history the chosen people of God (Al-Qur'an 16:36) and all can be now. It is an honor in which God bestows as a reward for your faith and works, not a birthright.

PROPHET LIKE MOSES (pbuh)

As I have stated, knowledge of the Qur'an will help you better understand the Jewish Torah.

Al-Qur'an 5:48 To thee We sent the Scripture in truth, confirming the scripture that came before it, and guarding it in safety: so judge between them (other scriptures) by what Allah hath revealed (the Qur'an)

The commonalities of the Qur'an and the Hebrew scriptures indicate to me that the Hebrew Scriptures were inspired by the original Torah. One prophecy in particular gives Muslims great pleasure to read. Jesus (pbuh) did not give credence to the authenticity of the Hebrew Scriptures, but he suggested that if his opponents read "their" scripture they would find reference to him. In the same vein, the Qur'an asks People of the book (Jews and Christians) to read their scriptures and they will find that Muhammad (pbuh) is mentioned in their books (7:157). The prophecy in questions is from Deuteronomy.

Deuteronomy 18:18 I will raise them up a prophet from among their brethren, like unto thee; and I will put My words in his mouth, and he shall speak unto them all that I shall command him.
Deuteronomy 18:19 And it shall come to pass, that whosoever will not hearken unto My words which he shall speak in My name, I will require it of him.

I must first note that this prophet is to be from among the brothers of the Israelite people. Had the prophecy been in reference to another Israelite prophet, it would have said "I will raise them up a prophet from among themselves" not "among their brethren." The Israelites are descendants of Israel former known as Jacob, who was Isaac's son (pbut). Isaac is Abraham's (pbut) second son. His first son was Ishmael (pbuh). Therefore all the descendants of Ishmael (pbuh) are the brethren of the Israelite people. And the descendants of the Ishmael (pbuh) or the Ishmaelite are the Arabs of today. And of course the prophet of Islam was an Arab by the name of Muhammad (pbuh) and he was definitely "like Moses" in that he was a messenger delivering a new code of ethics to his people, as well as liberator of the believers from those who sought them harm. Like Moses (pbuh), he was also a king, judge and jury over his people. Muhammad (pbuh) was also a general and soldier in war. Most certainly the phrase "I will put my words into his mouth" is an excellent description of how the revelation of God, Al-Qur'an, was given to Muhammad (pbuh). The first word spoken to Muhammad (pbuh) by the angel Jibril (Gabriel) was" Iqraa," which means to read or recite. Muhammad (pbuh) was obviously bewildered upon hearing this and even more confusing was the fact that he was illiterate and he thought he was being told to "read" something, when in fact he was to "recite" something. The angel gave him revelation and he was to recite and proclaim in to the world. In fact, much of the Qur'an comes in answer form as a direct response to questions or events surrounding the prophet of Islam. For example, Muhammad (pbuh) is asked to describe the nature of God by those surrounding him. In answer to this inquiry, God sends the angel to Muhammad (pbuh) telling him to

Al-Qur'an 112:1 Say: He is Allah, the One and Only;
Al-Qur'an 112:2 Allah, the Eternal, Absolute;
Al-Qur'an 112:3 He begetteth not, nor is He begotten;
Al-Qur'an 112:4 And there is none like unto Him.

God instructs Muhammad (pbuh) to "say" or "tell them" thus and so, giving his audience and the reader the understanding the words which he is speaking are not his own. They are "words put into his mouth" by God. It has been noted that the language of the Qur'an and the recorded words of Muhammad (pbuh) are in two different Arabic dialects. When Muhammad (pbuh) spoke on his own accord, it was quite distinct from the language, articulation, verbiage, tone, poetic rhyme, imagery, meaning and wisdom of the Qur'an. All these aspects of the Qur'an are unmatched to this very day by any literary work. The Qur'an revolutionized the Arabic language and it is the yardstick by which all the dialects of the language are measured, not to mention the miraculous nature of its contents. There have been volumes of books written about the scientific facts mentioned in the Qur'an, which no man of that time could have declared with as much certainty as Muhammad (pbuh). At this point, it is not imperative for you to believe that Muhammad (pbuh) actually received words from God, but that the description presented in Deuteronomy about the prophet with words put in his mouth, is the exact understanding that every Muslim on earth and since the time of Muhammad (pbuh) have had about him long before the Jewish Torah was even translated into Arabic.

The most important aspect of this prophecy is its ending. Its ending is a threat. If you do not listen and heed the message of this prophet, God says "I will require it of you." This phrase is also translated as "I will be the revenger." Ahmed Deedat, a champion of comparative religion, once alluded to the fear one has when he is confronted by a mugger. He contrasted this with the fear one should have when threatened by God Almighty. A prophecy which warrants God's emphasis on its importance should not be taken lightly. A Muslim looks at this threat as an indicator that the subject of this prophecy, Muhammad (pbuh), was given such great emphasis because he is the final messenger sent by God to the whole of mankind.

ACCUSATIONS OF PLAGIARISM

Because the Qur'an mentions several stories which are to be found in the Jewish Torah, many have suggested that Muhammad (pbuh) took his stories from the Bible of the Jews and Christians around him. As I have already mentioned, the scriptures were not translated into Arabic in the times of Prophet Muhammad (pbuh). This should be combined with the fact that like most people of that time, Prophet Muhammad (pbuh) could neither read nor write. (I believe that God chose an illiterate man in order to aid the Muslim in any argument suggesting that the Qur'an was plagiarized.)

Another key point to be made is that the Qur'an says that it is the criterion by which we judge other scriptures. In other words, it is the standard by which we distinguish the true from the false in other books. Therefore as a tool of measurement, it must be accurate itself. True to its proclamation, the Qur'an contains none of the errors mentioned in the Jewish Torah, though it describes some of the same events and characters. This would mean that even if Muhammad (pbuh) could read and knew several different languages (Hebrew, Arabic, Aramaic and Greek), he would still need assistance from God to make corrections where necessary. For example, the Qur'an explains the origin of the universe without making a single error of science, when the Jewish Torah has numerous mistakes on this subject. The Qur'an gives details on the orbit of the sun and moon and the light that they produce. Where did he get such information? And where did he get the confidence to say this is an absolute fact? He would also need assistance from God to correct the mistakes made on the life of the prophets from thousands of years before him. The list of impossibilities for Prophet Muhammad (pbuh) or any human being 1400 years ago to produce the Qur'an is innumerous.

But there are still those who would insist that Muhammad (pbuh) got his information from his travels or from his wife's cousin, Waraqa. This topic will be addressed further in my book, "Islam Is The Truth." But let us now simply state that Muhammad (pbuh) traveled outside of Mecca only three times, when he was 6, 12,and 25 years old. As for Waraqa, a very learned Arab Christian and the cousin of Muhammad's (pbuh) wife Khadijah, he and Muhammad (pbuh) met twice and on that second occasion, Muhammad (pbuh) was frighten after his first encounter with the angel Jibril, and Waraqa encouraged Muhammad (pbuh) to continue on because he believe Muhammad (pbuh) to be a true prophet of God. Though Waraqa died shortly afterwards, revelations to Muhammad (pbuh) continued on for 20 more years. If you add all the time Muhammad (pbuh) had outside of Mecca, with his Christian relative, with the probability for human error and forgetfulness, and the fact that Prophet Muhammad (pbuh) could not read or write, it is highly unlikely that Prophet Muhammad (pbuh) plagiarized the Qur'an. The only ground someone making this claim against Muhammad (pbuh) can stand upon is that Prophet Muhammad (pbuh) uses the same name and places mentioned in the Jewish Torah. If this is true then every dictionary, thesaurus and encyclopedia has plagiarized another. This is a clear misunderstanding of the definition of plagiarism.

Plagiarism: *the act of appropriating the literary composition of another author, or excerpts, ideas, or passages therefrom, and passing the material off as one's own creation*

The obvious mistake is that Prophet Muhammad (pbuh) never ever took credit for the Qur'an. The Qur'an explicitly says that it is from God and it claims that the text of these other scriptures is the work of men, who attribute their work to God. Thus if you read the Qur'an you will come to understand the truth in it and that it is a correction of the previous scripture.

Correction: *the act of offering an improvement to replace a mistake; setting right*

What I like to ask those who insist that the Qur'an is taken from the Bible is, "how can you correct something without mentioning it?" The Qur'an gives a conflicting story of Moses' (pbuh) request to see God as stated in the Jewish Torah. The Qur'an does not address the claim made in the Jewish Torah that Moses (pbuh) saw God's back parts. It's simply tells the real story. How can this story be told accurately without mentioning certain aspects contained in the Jewish Torah. You must mention Moses (pbuh), and Moses' (pbuh) request, God and God's reply and the outcome. In this instance, the outcome was the difference between the two scriptures. We must ask ourselves after the review of both the Qur'an and the Jewish Torah, which is more possible, probable, logical, reasonable and believable? Then we must ask ourselves, does the Qur'an do what it claims? Does it correct the scripture? Let us explore the similarities and differences in these scriptures.

DISTINCTIONS IN THE QUR'AN AND THE JEWISH TORAH

CREATION OF THE UNIVERSE

We find in the description of creation of the universe in the Jewish Torah several discrepancies with science. However as noted by Dr. Maurice Bacuille, the French scientist and author of the Book, "The Bible, the Qur'an and Science," these deficiencies do not occur in the Qur'an. Though the Qur'an uses the same verbiage as the Jewish Torah in its assessment of time required to create the universe, the author of the Qur'an did not use the words six days to literally mean six periods lasting 24 hours, as the Jewish Torah had. The Arabic word used for days is "yaum" which is used in this context as a long period of time. Therefore the Qur'anic point of view is that the universe was formed in six stages or periods, not six days and evenings as the Jewish Torah suggests.

To further illustrate this point the Qur'an gives examples of the relativity of time. It describes a person's perception of his lifetime on earth as feeling like a day or part of a day (Al-Qur'an 23:112-113). It also describes a day as being 10,000 years (Al-Qur'an 32:5) and the relativity of another "yaum" or day to be like 50,000 years (Al-Qur'an 70:4). The theory of relativity, for which Albert Einstein is known, was mentioned 1300 years before he was born in the Qur'an. Thus the six stages of creation might seem like billions of years to man, but they were but a moment to God. Ironically, in a debate between Ahmed Deedat and Rev. Jimmy Swaggert, entitled "Is the Bible God's Word," Mr. Swaggert cites the different descriptions of time in the Qur'an to be a mistake made by the author. From the title of the debate, it should be clear that he was intending to sway the audience to focus on anything other than the book in question, but in fact the explanation of the Qur'anic verses gives credence to its authenticity and degrades the authenticity of the Bible. Mr. Swaggert's examples merely showed that the author of the Qur'an was aware of the scientific fact that time is relative and that Muslims are not bound by the understanding that the universe was created in 144 hours as those who believe in the Jewish Torah are bound.

Another astounding fact about the Qur'an is that it describes the heavens (space and all its celestial body) and earth to be join together in its inception and then split apart (Al-Qur'an 21:30). One may notice the striking similarities this description has with modern science's "Big Bang Theory" in which the universe was one mass and it exploded and began to form into what is present today. Many people are reluctant to embrace this view because it is always coupled with the "theory of evolution," not realizing that simply because things are grouped together does not mean that they cannot be separately examined for their validity. The Qur'an suggests that the earth and the heavens were created simultaneously. This again frees those who believe in the Qur'an of the struggle of explaining how there was vegetation and light before the sun was formulated, as the Jewish Torah states.

Of great importance also, is the Qur'an's declaration that God neither sleeps nor slumbers and he feels no fatigue (Al-Qur'an 2:255). This sentiment by the Qur'an contradicts the idea that God rests and was refreshed on the day after creation (Ex. 31:17).

CREATION OF MAN

The second chapter of Genesis says that God created man from dust, however the author of the Qur'an expounds upon this claim. The Qur'an says man is created from several different elements and just as Mr. Swaggert attempted to discredit the Qur'an, so too does many others claim that the Qur'an is in conflict with itself about the contents used to create man. And as with Mr. Swaggert, their haste to find an error only helps the credibility of the Qur'an when examined carefully. It is often asked of Muslims, "did God create man from dust (Al-Qur'an 30:20), clay (Al-Qur'an 15:26), water (Al-Qur'an 25:54), the word 'be' (Al-Qur'an 3:47) or from nothing (Al-Qur'an 19:67)?" The Muslim is obliged to simply place their list in the proper order, so they will better understand the Qur'an's more detailed description of man's creation. At one point, no man existed. From nothing, God willed man into existence by his word "be" and man began to form from water and the dust or soil of the earth. The mixture formed into solid clay in which God breathed life. The Qur'an goes on to describe the birth of a child as an embryo in the womb of a woman, without the assistance of any modern medical or scientific instruments, most notably a microscope.

Al-Qur'an 4:1 O mankind! reverence your Guardian-Lord, who created you from a single nafs(soul or being), created, of like nature, His mate, and from them twain scattered (like seeds) countless men and women;- reverence Allah, through whom ye demand your mutual (rights), and (reverence) the wombs (That bore you): for Allah ever watches over you.

If we remember in Genesis the story of Cain, it indicates that there were more people on earth besides him, his deceased brother, Adam (pbuh) and Eve. However there is no further mention of these people. The sole focus on Adam (pbuh) and Eve's children have led many who believe in the Jewish Torah to adopt the notion that incest was permissible in the beginning of creation. And this incest is the cause by which the earth is populated. If we are to take a look at the Qur'anic message above, it provides an answer to the existence of those mysterious people and to how the world was populated. The verse is in reference to the creation of Adam (pbuh) and Eve. The words "countless man and women" is directly speaking of mankind. I believe this "countless men and women" are those whom God created from Adam (pbuh) and Eve and scattered all over the earth.

Al-Qur'an 49:13 O mankind! We created you from a single (pair) of a male and a female, and made you into nations and tribes, that ye may know each other (not that ye may despise (each other). Verily the most honoured of you in the sight of Allah is (he who is) the most righteous of you. And Allah has full knowledge and is well acquainted (with all things).

This understanding of man's creation negates the necessity for incest. This would mean that we are all the children of Adam (pbuh) and Eve in a sense, but Cain and Abel were his children through the natural process. God spread mankind about the earth like he did the planets of the universe and they began to multiply.

The Qur'an is in agreement with the Jewish Torah in the pronouncement that God breathed his spirit into man, but it rejects the literal interpretation of man being in God's image. Man is made pure and he is to strive in his life to remain or regain that state of purity. Purity and righteousness is the image of God given to man.

ADAM (pbuh) AND EVE

The transgression of Adam (pbuh) and Eve is also recorded in the Qur'an. There is no mention of a serpent, but there is mention of satan whispering suggestions of disobedience to the two. The Jewish Torah leaves the reader in the dark about the identity of this serpent. It is through some interpretation of other scriptures and tradition that we find the serpent was actually satan. The Qur'an says that satan misled Adam (pbuh) and his wife by deceiving them. He told them that God did not want them to eat from the tree because they would be like ANGELS or immortals. This of course is not true because they were at that time immortal and already superior to the angels (Al-Qur'an 7:11). On the other hand, the Jewish Torah says that satan told them the truth, when he said that they will be like God, knowing good and evil. The Jewish Torah also depicts the couple as frolicking naked around the garden. It says that they were unaware or unashamed of their nakedness until after they sinned (Genesis 2:25, 3:7). The Qur'an tells a different story.

Al-Qur'an 7:26 O ye Children of Adam! We have bestowed raiment upon you to cover your shame, as well as to be an adornment to you. But the raiment of righteousness,- that is the best. Such are among the Signs of Allah, that they may receive admonition! Al-Qur'an 7:27 O ye Children of Adam! Let not Satan seduce you, in the same manner as He got your parents out of the Garden, stripping them of their raiment, to expose their shame

It appears that raiment or clothing can be taken literally or figuratively. If it is taken literally, then the Qur'an contests the idea that they were walking about nude until after they sinned. The Qur'an says that they were clothed and satan "stripped them of their raiment." The Qur'an is also free of the indignity given to God in the Jewish Torah. The story of Adam (pbuh) and Eve does not contain images of God being unable to find his creation. There is also the absent of the passing of the buck to one another. The Qur'an maintains that Adam (pbuh) and Eve both accepted their responsibility for their sin and they repented (Al-Qur'an 7:23). In fact, they are forgiven by God in the Qur'an (Al-Qur'an 2:37). The only stipulation was that they were to be tested on earth to earn their way to Paradise. There is no mention of a cursed or punishment placed on all men and women because of the acts of two individuals. Man will work in hard labor while women will give birth in hard labor are not a result of the sins of Adam (pbuh) and Eve. I would assume that they are not to be understood as punishment but a test of the struggle and the will of men and women to help them to better appreciate the positive results of their labor. Another major distinction is that the Qur'an ranks Adam (pbuh) as a prophet appointed by God to mankind (Al-Qur'an 20:122).

NOAH (pbuh)

Of great importance is the character of a messenger of God. Muslims hold the prophets of God in the highest regard that a human being can be placed. The idea that Noah (pbuh), a man chosen by God over everyone else, was in a drunken stupor and cursed his grandchildren is one unfathomable by Muslims. Man's standards of delegating an official spokesman would not permit him to appoint a man of this sort. So how likely is it that God would appoint a man with very questionable character and judgment? It would seem reasonable that had Noah (pbuh) made such a spectacle of himself and placed a curse on the innocent, at the very less, God would have admonition him for these things. Intoxicates are prohibited in Islam (Al-Qur'an 5:90-91) as in some parts of the Bible. And the Qur'an asserts that "no one can bear the burden of another" (Al-Qur'an 17:15) and the Jewish Torah does, as well. There is no curse handed down to children for the transgressions of their parents.

Another interesting correction made in the Qur'an is that the flood was not a global flood as described in the Bible (Gen. 7:4) but a local flood which only drowned Noah's (pbuh) rebellious people (Al-Qur'an 7:64). Many scholars of the Jewish Torah have attempted to prove that the flood described in the Jewish Torah was local because of the improbability of a global flood to occur, especially without significant amounts of evidence to support it, but the text of Genesis is their nemesis in this battle. It is clear that the author is describing a global flood, as it uses the same word for earth in Noah's (pbuh) story as was used in Genesis 1:1.

ABRAHAM (pbuh), HAGAR AND ISHMAEL (pbuh)

It would seem that Jews and Christians prefer to call the father of their faiths, Abraham, an adulterer, which is a crime punishable by death, than to give Hagar and her son, Ishmael (pbut), legitimacy. In Islamic tradition as in the Jewish Torah, it is made clear that Hagar and Sarah were both the wives of Abraham (pbuh). The Qur'an records no bickering or dislike between the two. Some Muslim scholars suggests that Hagar was not a handmaid (Gen. 16:1) or a slave (Gen. 21:12) at all but she was an Egyptian princess, purposely belittled by the Jewish Torah's author, perhaps because she was from the country which enslaved the Israelites. Also The Qur'an mentions the departure of Hagar and Ishmael (pbuh) as a decision made by God and not at the whims of a jealous wife. ALLAH is called "the best of planners" in the Qur'an (3:54) and it is obvious that his plan was to raise from the lineage of Hagar and Ishmael the successor to Jesus Christ, the "prophet like Moses" and the final messenger to mankind, Prophet Muhammad (pbut).

In an effort to downplay anyone other than those in direct relations to the children of Israel and to exalt the position of Israel's father, Isaac (pbuh), the author of the Jewish Torah commits several mistakes. Muslims understand the willingness of Abraham to sacrifice his son to God as a testament to his complete submission to the will of God, yet they believe the son to be Ishmael, whereas the Jewish Torah specifically says that Isaac (pbut) was the son to be sacrificed.

In order to recognize the error in this story of the Jewish Torah, we must first examine the time at which these events were said to have occurred and the age of those involved. The problem the Jewish Torah's author has is that during the sacrifice, Isaac is called Abraham's (pbut) "only son" three times (Gen. 22:2, 12, 16). Yet it is well known and documented that Ishmael (pbuh) was the first son to be born because Sarah was barren. Not to mention the fact that the Jewish Torah calls Ishmael (pbuh) "his son" on numerous occasions, which nullifies the claim that he was illegitimate?

Ishmael is the son who could have been called "thine only son," but this story is said to have occurred after the birth of Isaac (pbut). This puts the authenticity of the Jewish Torah into another twist, because Ishmael (pbuh) could not be the only son either. But as I have said when you study the Qur'an and Islam, the stories of the Jewish Torah become clearer. In an effort to take Ishmael and his mother out of the equation when it came to the inheritance of Abraham, the author tells the story of Ishmael teasing his brother, Isaac and his mother, Sarah, commanding Abraham to exile Hagar and Ishmael (pbut) to the desert. As I have stated the Qur'an makes no mention of such matters, but it says that God made this pronouncement and Sarah is not mentioned at all.

Instead, God's motive was to have Ishmael and Abraham (pbut) build the Kaaba and establish prayer there (Al-Qur'an 14:37). This is a much more noble and godlike reason than the one given in the Jewish Torah. The story in Genesis seems to be a fabrication which would cause a permanent rift between the two brothers and their descendants.

We read in the Jewish Torah that when Hagar and Ishmael (pbuh) were sent away, they both were near death for thirst. But the problem with the story is that Hagar is said to have carried the lad on her back through the wilderness. The author did not realize that Ishmael (pbuh) was 16 years old at this time. When the covenant was given to Abraham, he was 99 and Ishmael (pbut) was 13 (Gen. 17:23-25). When Abraham was 100 yrs old, Isaac (pbut) was born (Gen. 21:5), making Ishmael 14. And it was stated that Isaac was weaning when Ishmael (pbut) and Hagar were exiled (Gen. 21:8, 10), adding about two years to Isaac and Ishmael's (pbuh) age. So can we assume that Hagar took bread, water and a 16 year old child on her back and carried him through the wilderness until their sustenance ran dry? At this point, "she cast the child under one of the shrubs "(Gen. 21:15). It is apparent that this child is a baby or a toddler, not a 16 year old boy. At age 16, Ishmael (pbuh) would have been more of a help than a liability. In any case, Hagar became distressed and began crying and calling to God. But what is noteworthy is that God did not answer her prayers, but the prayers of the child were answered (Gen. 21:17), because Ishmael (pbuh) literally means God hears (prayers). And God sent them an angel, who gave them a well of water to drink and they were saved.

There are a few things we need to take from this story. First is the understanding that it is chronologically out of place because it occurs long before Isaac was born because Ishmael (pbut) was a small child at the time, thus the story of the teasing, Sarah's jealousy and God conforming to her whims were fabrications. But why does this happen? Why would a story be fabricated like this?

The answer comes in the very next chapter. In chapter 22, we have the story of the sacrifice and the author must place Isaac (pbuh) at the scene, even though he is probably several years removed from the event. Yet in the covenant given to Abraham (pbuh), God says it is with Abraham (pbuh) and his seed. Despite the fact that Ishmael was the firstborn and he was circumcised at this very time, the author specifies that the covenant is with Isaac (pbut). He does the same thing when the mother and son are exiled. God comforts Abraham about the departure of his family, by saying that the covenant is with Isaac (pbut) (Gen. 21:12). It is first irrational to think that such a promise helps ease the pain of a father losing his wife and son. Secondly, Isaac (pbuh) was again 14 years away from being born. This coupled with the law that the firstborn is to receive double the inheritance of the other sons (Deut. 21:15-17) shows that the author went through great pains to give Isaac the blessings that the laws of God had ordained Ishmael (pbut) to receive. And as the first son and the son whom Abraham (pbuh) had longed for, it is apparent that he would be the son to test the sincerity of Abraham (pbuh) through sacrifice.

Some say that Isaac was the only son that Abraham loved, in order to grant Isaac some degree over Ishmael (pbut). In their effort to downgrade Ishmael, they have in effect degraded their beloved Abraham (pbut) when they suggest that he does not love his own son. But this claim holds no weight at all when we remember how saddened Abraham was to send his son, Ishmael (pbut), away. Abraham is distraught when he is told that Ishmael (pbut) must leave. Abraham had deep feelings for Ishmael (pbut). When God announced Isaac's birth , the first person Abraham thought of was Ishmael, as if to say, thank you for this blessing but don't forget my eldest son Ishmael (pbut) (Gen 17:18). It would appear that the God of the Jewish Torah did not share the same fondness for the child.

The Jewish Torah describes the annunciation of Ishmael's (pbuh) birth. An angel came to console Hagar because of the harsh treatment she had received from Sarah (Gen.16: 7-8). He gave her news of a son, Ishmael (pbuh), his name meaning "God hears," "because HaShem hath heard thy affliction." Yet even in this moment of glad tidings from God, the author of the Jewish Torah must not let the reader feel favorable towards this "child sent by God." The angel goes on to describe Ishmael (pbuh).

Genesis 16:12 And he shall be a wild ass of a man: his hand shall be against every man, and every man's hand against him; and he shall dwell in the face of all his brethren.

Is this the way in which comforting is to be performed, by belittling and incriminating an unborn child? This is an obvious attempt to degrade Ishmael (pbuh) as soon as his name is mentioned. The proof that this verse is untrue and placed here with an ulterior motive is the fact that

Hagar does not even acknowledge the claims made about her unborn son. She is in a fragile state to begin with. To add the insulting of her child BY GOD ALMIGHTY would send her into frenzy. But on the contrary, she rejoices and sends praise to God for the news (Gen. 16:13).

We can see from the annunciation of Ishmael's (pbuh) birth and his near death experience that the portrayal of Hagar and Ishmael (pbuh) in the Jewish Torah as inferior to their counterparts (Sarah and Isaac) has been purposely done. To what rank of honor do we give a woman whose cries are immediately heard, addressed and answered by God? This is a distinction given to prophets of God. God was compelled to send his angel to console this woman. How on earth can she be deemed inferior to someone like Sarah, who laughs at the possibility of a miracle from God (Gen.18:12- 15)? In like manner, her son Ishmael's (pbuh) voice was heard by God and God delivered him from harm through his own angel. Just as Israel's name denotes the struggle that he had with God throughout his life, the name Ishmael (pbuh) denotes that God will hear and answer his prayers throughout his life. How can such a man be "a wild ass of a man?"

In Islam, Ishmael is a prophet of God and similar to the annunciation of the birth of Jesus, Ishmael's (pbut) birth was announced by an angel. His call to God was heard and answered because he was God's prophet. The well of water that the angel directed him and his mother to is well known in Islam as the well of Zam Zam, which still runs to this day. The place in which they settled in the Jewish Torah called Paran (Gen. 21:21) is now known as Mecca. But unlike the Jewish Torah which suggests that Abraham abandoned his wife and child, in Islam Abraham and Ishmael (pbut) were quite close. The Kaaba which is where every Muslim on earth faces to pray was built by Abraham and his son, Ishmael (pbut) in Mecca.
I must also state that there is no firstborn right in Islam and Ishmael and Isaac (pbut) were both good brothers and prophets of God in Islam. Muslims are not to make any distinctions between prophets. I intend to show no superiority of Ishmael over Isaac or vice versa, merely to establish the fact that the character of Ishmael (pbut) and Hagar has long been degraded and it is about time they get the credit that they deserve. In an effort to dismiss and discredit Ishmael (pbuh) and his descendants, the author of the Jewish Torah has even done a disservice to his own hero. Abraham (pbuh), the patriarch of the Israelites, is accused on enslaving an Egyptian (Hagar) long before Egyptians enslaved Israelites.

ABRAHAM'S (pbuh) SACRIFICE IN THE QUR'AN

Al-Qur'an 37:99 He (Abraham) said: "I will go to my Lord! He will surely guide me!

Al-Qur'an 37:100 "O my Lord! Grant me a righteous (son)!"

Al-Qur'an 37:101 So We gave him the good news of a boy ready to suffer and forbear.

Al-Qur'an 37:102 Then, when (the son) reached (the age of) (serious) work with him, he said: "O my son! I see in vision that I offer thee in sacrifice: Now see what is thy view!" (The son) said: "O my father! Do as thou art commanded: thou will find me, if Allah so wills one practicing Patience and Constancy!"

Al-Qur'an 37:103 So when they had both submitted their wills (to Allah), and he had laid him prostrate on his forehead (for sacrifice),

Al-Qur'an 37:104 We called out to him "O Abraham!

Al-Qur'an 37:105 "Thou hast already fulfilled the vision!" - thus indeed do We reward those who do right.

Al-Qur'an 37:106 For this was obviously a trial-

Al-Qur'an 37:107 And We ransomed him with a momentous sacrifice:

Al-Qur'an 37:108 And We left (this blessing) for him among generations (to come) in later times:

Al-Qur'an 37:109 "Peace and salutation to Abraham!"

Al-Qur'an 37:110 Thus indeed do We reward those who do right.

Al-Qur'an 37:111 For he was one of our believing Servants.

Al-Qur'an 37:112 And We gave him the good news of Isaac - a prophet,- one of the Righteous.

The Qur'an puts the stories of the prophets and their endeavors in a nutshell. As seen in the verses above, the Qur'an gives the gist of stories only to convey that the most important aspect of the story is the display of submission to God. The Qur'an makes it clear here that the son is of mature age and that he is just as willing as Abraham (pbuh) is to do as God commands. While in the Qur'an, Abraham (pbuh) is upfront with his son about his vision to have him sacrificed, the Jewish Torah would have us to believed that Abraham (pbuh) lied to his son.

Genesis 22:7 And Isaac spoke unto Abraham his father, and said: 'My father.' And he said: 'Here am I, my son.' And he said: 'Behold the fire and the wood; but where is the lamb for a burnt offering?'
Genesis 22:8 And Abraham said: 'G-d will provide Himself the lamb for a burnt-offering, my son.' So they went both of them together.

Here Isaac specifically asks his father where is the sacrificial animal and Abraham, believing that Isaac (pbut) was to be the actual sacrifice, told him that there will be a lamb to sacrifice provided by God. Of course, Isaac's (pbuh) death was halted by an angel of God and a ram was offered to God instead of his son (Gen. 22:13). This might compel some to assume that Abraham (pbuh) was not lying to his son. The problem with the idea that Abraham (pbuh) already knew that a ram would be substituted is that this episode would not really be a test to prove Abraham's (pbuh) faith as the Jewish Torah suggests (Gen. 22:1-2, 12). So the Jewish Torah depicts this prophet as untruthful, even to his son in his last moments on earth. Even worse is that Abraham, tied and bound Isaac (pbut) according to the Jewish Torah (Gen. 22:9). Can you imagine the terror that Isaac (pbuh) felt when he finally realized that his father has lied to him and he is to be the sacrifice? Compare this to the words of Ishmael (pbuh) in the Qur'an:

Al-Qur'an 37:102 "O my father! Do as thou art commanded: thou will find me, if Allah so wills one practicing Patience and Constancy!"

Though the principle of the story is basically the same in the Jewish Torah and the Qur'an, to submit your will to God, but the Qur'anic version of the sacrificial son is much more noble and believable as it pertains to men of God. The Qur'an puts more emphasis on their submission to God, than it does on the identity of the participants. While it does not say that this son is Ishmael (pbuh), it gives us hints to draw this conclusion. It is easily deduced from the verses of chapter 37:99-102 that the son which Abraham (pbuh) prayed for, the son whom God granted him and the sacrificial son were all one in the same. Also this son is described as one who "practices patience and constancy." It is no coincidence that Ishmael (pbuh) is again described with these exact attributes in another place in the Quran, 21:85. The final bit of evidence is the sequence of events described in the Quran. Abraham (pbuh) asks for a son. He is granted a son. Abraham (pbuh) is tested. Then Isaac (pbuh) is born.

As the Qur'an says of itself, it is the criteria by which other scriptures are to be judged. When you read the Qur'an, you will better understand the Jewish Torah.

LOT (pbuh)

Lot (pbuh) was living amongst the sinful inhabitants of Sodom and Gomorrah. He was summoned by God to have his people repent from

their sins and lead a righteous life, but they refused. In the Jewish Torah's narrative, God and 2 angels come to earth to assess the situation (Gen. 18:21). They first arrive at Abraham's (pbuh) home. There he has a meal prepared and GOD ALMIGHTY and his angels ate and drank with Abraham (pbuh). Then they are off to the land of Sodom and Gomorrah. On the way there, Abraham (pbuh)stops and pleads with God to spare the lives of the inhabitants. Through a lengthy negotiation process, GOD ALMIGHTY agrees with Abraham's (pbuh) terms to spare the people if he finds 10 righteous people in the land (Gen. 18:23-32). Unfortunately for the people of Sodom and Gomorrah, there were not even 10 righteous people in the land. So God had Lot (pbuh), his wife and two daughters escorted out of the city, and he had the city destroyed. But Lot's (pbuh) wife looked back at the destroyed city and she was turned into a pillar of salt (Gen. 19:26).
Here is the Qur'anic view of the same event.

Al-Qur'an 29:28 And (remember) Lut: behold, he said to his people: "Ye do commit lewdness, such as no people in Creation (ever) committed before you.
Al-Qur'an 29:29 "Do ye indeed approach men, and cut off the highway?- and practise wickedness (even) in your councils?" But his people gave no answer but this: they said: "Bring us the Wrath of Allah if thou tellest the truth."
Al-Qur'an 29:30 He said: "O my Lord! help Thou me against people who do mischief!"
Al-Qur'an 29:31 When Our Messengers came to Abraham with the good news, they said: "We are indeed going to destroy the people of this township: for truly they are (addicted to) crime."
Al-Qur'an 29:32 He said: "But there is Lut there." They said: "Well do we know who is there: we will certainly save him and his following,- except his wife: she is of those who lag behind!"

Al-Qur'an 29:33 And when Our Messengers came to Lut, he was grieved on their account, and felt himself powerless (to protect) them: but they said: "Fear thou not, nor grieve: we are (here) to save thee and thy following, except thy wife: she is of those who lag behind.

Al-Qur'an 29:34 "For we are going to bring down on the people of this township a Punishment from heaven, because they have been wickedly rebellious."

Al-Qur'an 29:35 And We have left thereof an evident Sign, for any people who (care to) understand

First we notice that God is not visiting Abraham (pbuh) at all. His messengers (angels) were. The story of the angels visit to Abraham's (pbuh) home is described in two places in the Qur'an (11:69-70, 51:24-31) and both agree that the angels did not eat the food Abraham (pbuh) had prepared for them. Though they appeared to be human, they had no need for earthly food. They were sent on a mission to destroy the city, not to determine whether it was deemed suitable to be destroyed. Also, the crimes that Sodom and Gomorrah committed were not only acts of homosexuality but also kidnapping, holding people hostage and rape. Both the Qur'an and the Jewish Torah attest to the people intending on raping the angels, as they thought them to be men, but the Qur'an suggests that that they "cut off the highway (or road)." This gives the impression that they captured and held captive its travelers. This gives a better understanding as to why God punished them so harshly.

In the Jewish Torah, Abraham bargains with God to save Lot's (pbut) people. These people were of a different race and religion from Abraham (pbuh), yet he unlike the author of the Jewish Torah felt compassion towards non-Jews. In the Qur'an, God was not onsite to argue with Abraham, but Abraham did beg the angels to save Lot's (pbut) people. However it was no negotiations. God did not second guess his decision. It was decreed that those savage people be punished. The angels say:

Al-Qur'an 11:76 O Abraham! Seek not this. The decree of thy Lord hath gone forth: for them there cometh a penalty that cannot be turned back!

One would expect that the wisdom and justice of God would not be so inferior to man that God reconsiders his position. The Jewish Torah's version of the events would have us to believe that God had not fully assessed the situation and that punishment might not be warranted. The Qur'an stands in sharp contrast to such an idea.

Furthermore, the Jewish Torah mentions that Lot (pbuh) offered his 2 daughters to the crazed men of Sodom (Gen 19:8). The Qur'an also makes mention of this scene with Lot and the hostile crowd.

Al-Quran 11:78 He (Lot) said, "O my people, these are my daughters; they are purer for you.

Since the Qur'an is the correction of the Jewish Torah, we must be careful not to pass over seemingly small nuances between the two narratives. Notice that the Qur'an does not say that Lot (pbuh) gave his "TWO daughters" as the Jewish Torah does. The Qur'an says "daughters" and "they." Now we must bear in mind that Arabic has a single form, a dual form, and a plural form (3 or more) of nouns and pronouns. The words for "daughter" and "they," in the Qur'an, do not use the dual form, but the plural form. This indicates that Lot (pbuh) recommended that the men of the crowd seek companionship with Lot's figurative daughters, i.e. the women of the city of Sodom, not his actual 2 daughters which according to the Jewish Torah were already married. Also the Qur'an is void of an incestuous relationship between a drunken Lot (pbuh) and his daughters. Once again, the Qur'an rescues the character of a Prophet of God.

Another distinction is that the Qur'an explains that it was never intended for Lot's (pbuh) wife to be saved from punishment. She wished to be amongst the sin of the people of city. This gives a better understanding to her punishment, and the claim that she simply looked back at the city and she was consumed (Gen. 19:26). If looking back was her only infraction then what should have happened to Lot (pbuh). He lingered around long after he was told to leave according to the Jewish Torah. Not only that, he had to be carried by the angels out of the city (Gen. 19:16). Would this not qualify Lot to be turned to a pillar of salt also?

The Qur'an in one instant describes Lot's (pbuh) wife as an old woman (Al-Quran 26:170-171). It has been the prerogative of some to attack such a description as insensitive or insulting, when in fact it is just the opposite. In Islamic culture, a man over the age of 50 is called sheikh to emphasize his wisdom and knowledge due to his life's learning and experience. It is presumed that one's life is not spent frivolously, thus he or she has a decent grasp of right and wrong and truth and falsehood. The word sheikh literally means "elder" or "old man," yet it is a title of endearment and honor. The Qur'an's description of Lot's (pbuh) wife as "an old woman" indicates that she, not only as a prophet's wife, but as an elder should have known the truth when it was presented to her.

JOSEPH (pbuh)

The story of Joseph (pbuh) in the Qur'an and the Jewish Torah has slight but important differences. We read in the Jewish Torah that Joseph (pbuh) is given the gift of interpreting dreams by God. He himself has a dream of eleven stars, the sun and the moon prostrating to him. He tells this dream to his father, Jacob (pbuh) or Israel, and his eleven brothers. It is apparent that the dream is in reference to the brothers, the father and mother paying homage to Joseph (pbuh). So, the TWELVE become incensed by the idea. His father rebuked him and his brothers sought to kill him. First they cast him into a well. Then, Judah felt they should gain a profit for their brother, so they sold him. The brothers went home and made their father believe that Joseph (pbuh) was killed by a wild animal. Jacob (pbuh) was completely distraught (Gen. 37:33-34). Eventually Joseph (pbuh) was given to Potiphar, an officer of the pharaoh's and captain of the guard.

As a servant of Potiphar, Joseph (pbuh) was admired by Potiphar's wife. So much so that she sought to seduce him. Being a pious man, he rejected her advances. But she was very persistent and on one occasion, she ripped his garment as he attempted to avoid being alone with her. Feeling anger from rejection, she falsely charged him with rape and she used his garment as proof of the incident (Gen. 39:16-18). Potiphar believed her allegation and put Joseph (pbuh) in prison.

In prison, he became famous for his dream interpreting abilities, to such an extent that he is summoned by the pharaoh to interpret the pharaoh's dream. He of course does so, thus gaining his freedom and a high position as confidant of the pharaoh. The pharaoh's dream is indicative of a future food shortage in the land and Joseph (pbuh) is put in charge of the rationing and selling of food. Inevitably, Jacob (pbuh) sends his 10 sons (without Benjamin) to buy food. Joseph (pbuh) recognizes his brothers, but they do not recognize him. The Jewish Torah then makes mention of Joseph (pbuh) remembering his dream (Gen. 42:9). And Joseph (pbuh), being close to his brother Benjamin, wished to see him. So he devised a plan to have the brothers bring Benjamin back. The plan works and when all the brothers are reunited, Joseph (pbuh) reveals to them who he is and he chalked all his adversity up to God's plan to give him rule over Egypt. News of their reuniting spread throughout the house of the pharaoh and the pharaoh rejoiced and gave the family of his riches. But the dream which Joseph (pbuh) had is never fulfilled.

The gist of the story is similar in the Qur'an, but the differences are profound. First off, the Qur'an never references to Jacob (pbuh) as Israel. There is no mention of this name change or the event in which it is said to have occurred. Secondly, the Qur'an lists Jacob and Joseph (pbuh) as prophets of God (Al-Qur'an 12:5-6, 21-22, 19:49-50). Therefore they both received revelation from God. This would explain why the Qur'an says that Joseph told Jacob of his dream and Jacob (pbut) immediately deemed it as a sign from God. This is in contrast to the anger he displays in the Jewish Torah. The Qur'an also hints at that mindstate of Joseph and Jacob (pbut). Joseph (pbuh) is presented as maybe being disturbed by his dream. He starts telling Jacob (pbuh) of the dream with "O my father" (12:4), which demonstrates his humility. And Jacob comforts Joseph (pbuh) with:

Al-Qur'an 12:5 "O my son, do not relate your vision to your brothers, lest they devise a plan against you; surely the Shaitan is an open enemy to man."

We see here that Joseph (pbuh) did not tell his brothers of the dream. Yet they plotted against him because they felt their father showed Joseph (pbuh) and Benjamin favoritism. So they put him in a well, but the Qur'an reveals that God spoke to Joseph (pbuh) in the well and told him that he will not die and that he will one day confront them for what they did (Al-Qur'an 12:15). As in the Jewish Torah, the brothers attempted to cover up their crime, but unlike the Jewish Torah, Jacob (pbuh) was not fooled. The Jewish Torah suggests Jacob (pbuh) was a man attuned to God, yet God leaves him in ignorance and mourning over his son's death. As a prophet of God and one in communication with God, the Qur'an asserts that Jacob (pbuh) knew their claims to be false and Jacob (pbuh) said," in time the truth will be revealed" (Al- Qur'an 12:18). Eventually a caravan of travelers (there is no dispute over who they were) came by and pulled Joseph (pbuh) from the well. They sold him to a man called "Al-Aziz" meaning "the exalted one." This is the description of the position this man held under the pharaoh. The Jewish Torah calls this man, Potiphar. At any rate, Al-Aziz's wife is smitten by Joseph (pbuh) and she wishes to become intimate with him. The Qur'an begins to elaborate on the event which occurred between Joseph (pbuh) and Al-Aziz's wife.

Al-Aziz's wife rips Joseph's (pbuh) shirt as he was attempting to get away from her and her advances. At which time, her husband was at the door. He believed Joseph (pbuh) was the one trying to seduce his wife. But a witness to the event said Joseph was innocent. They stated that if Joseph's (pbuh) shirt had been torn from the front, it would be that he was attempting a lewd act upon Al-Aziz's wife. But Joseph's (pbuh) shirt was torn from behind, corroborating his claim that he was not the pursuer, but that he was being pursued. There is no mention of this exoneration of Joseph (pbuh) in the Jewish Torah.

Al-Aziz's wife again sought to seduce Joseph (pbuh) and she threatened him with imprisonment if he did not concede. Joseph (pbuh), however, thought it more suitable to go to prison than to disobey the tenants of God's law by committing adultery. And he sought strength from God to help him remain on the straight path. While in prison, he discusses the oneness of God with prisoners and he eventually becomes well-known for his interpretation of dreams. At the behest of the KING, Joseph (pbuh) is summoned to become a confidant of the KING'S and he has authority over the storehouse. His brothers come to him but they did not recognize him, yet Joseph (pbuh) recognized them. He asked them to bring their youngest brother, Benjamin. They went back home to their father Jacob, and requested that they return to Joseph (pbut) with their younger brother. At which point, Jacob begins sobbing over Joseph (pbut), to such an extent that he lost his sight. The brothers are perturbed, wondering when Jacob will get over Joseph's (pbut) death. Jacob's (pbuh) says that he only sobs to God and that he "knew what they knew not." After returning to Joseph (pbuh) with Benjamin, Joseph (pbuh) finally tells them who he is. His brothers confess their sins and they acknowledge that God favored Joseph (pbuh) because of his righteous nature. Joseph (pbuh) sends his brothers, with his shirt as proof, to tell their father of the happenings. And Jacob's vision is miraculously restored by Joseph's (pbut) shirt. Jacob, himself, reveals that he knew that Joseph (pbut) was alive all the time, for God had informed him. Noticeable, in the Quran, is the brothers' need for forgiveness from God. The king's reaction to the family reunion is insignificant. And the story ends with both Joseph's (pbuh) parents and his brothers paying homage to him on his throne, just as the dream he had suggested.

When reading the Biblical and Qur'anic version of the story of Joseph (pbuh), we will notice several differences. The first is that the prophecy of the dream is fulfilled in the Qur'an, but not in the Jewish Torah. This is precisely because it is impossible for it to be fulfilled in the Jewish Torah, without discrediting Joseph (pbuh) or discrediting the Jewish Torah. Joseph (pbuh) dreamed of 11 stars, the sun and moon prostrating to him. That is his father, mother and 11 brothers. The problem is that the Jewish Torah says that his mother died while given birth to the youngest brother.

Genesis 35:18 And it came to pass, as her soul was in departing--for she died--that she called his name Ben-oni; but his father called him Benjamin.

Genesis 35:19 And Rachel died, and was buried in the way to Ephrath--the same is Beth-lehem.

This made the need for the author to ignore the dream of Joseph (pbuh). The Qur'an makes no such mistake and places both parents at the throne of Joseph (pbuh). Since the Jewish Torah has no mention of the fulfillment of the dream, it is very unlikely that the Qur'an was copied from the Jewish Torah. Another difference in the stories is the understanding of a prophet of God. Joseph and Jacob (pbuh) as prophets of God are not left in the dark about each other's situation. In the Qur'an, Jacob understood Joseph's dream immediately and Joseph (pbut) is aware of his father's ailment and its cure without his brothers making any mention of it. The anachronisms of Joseph's (pbuh) story in the Jewish Torah also attract attention. Earlier, I wrote about the Egyptians not dining with Hebrews as an anachronisms but the use of the words "Potiphar" and "Potiphera" as names in Joseph's story are problems as well. Some scholar believe this to be a title and not a personal name because the personal name "Potiphar" and "Potiphera," both mentioned in the Jewish Torah's account, were "not present in Egyptian records until well into the New kingdom, whereas Joseph's story occurs in the middle kingdom." - *http://www.islamicawareness.org/Quran/Contrad/External/aziz.html*

However the Bible uses them as names of people. The Qur'an does not contain this error. In that same vein, the title "pharaoh" is an anachronism also. In the time of Joseph (pbuh) (and Abraham), the rulers were not called pharaohs, but kings. In the time of Moses (pbuh) and thereafter, the rulers were called pharaohs. So when the Jewish Torah was written, it placed the word "pharaoh" in a time and place where it was not used. Perhaps the author was not intentionally misleading the audience, but merely using a word understandable to the audience. In contrast, the Qur'an, when speaking of Joseph's (pbuh) time, uses the word "malik" or king, but in the time of Moses (pbuh), it uses the word "firawn" or pharaoh. Of course, this makes the narrative in the Qur'an more accurate, but it does something else. It shames those who claim that Prophet Muhammad (pbuh) copied the Jewish Torah.

"The historicity of the Pharaonic title provides yet another sharp reminder to those that adhere to the precarious theory that parts of the Qur'an

were allegedly copied from the Bible. If Egyptian hieroglyphs were long dead and the biblical account an inaccurate work of folk memory, then from where did the Prophet Muhammad obtain his information? The Qur'an answers: Your Companion is neither astray nor being misled. Nor does he say (aught) of (his own) desire. It is no less than inspiration sent down to him. He was taught by one mighty in Power. [Qur'an 53:2-5]
-http://www.islamicawareness.org/Quran/Contrad/External/josephdetail.html

MOSES (pbuh)

His Birth

On the subject of Moses (pbuh), the Qur'an makes mention of the circumstances surrounding his birth. The Qur'an maintains that God inspired his mother to put Moses (pbuh) in a chest and put him in the river. The Jewish Torah says that Moses' mother "saw that he was a goodly child" (Ex. 2:2). The Qur'an says that God promised her that He will return Moses (pbuh) to her and that he will be God's messenger (Al-Qur'an 28:7). Therefore the reasoning behind his mother putting him into the river is not that she simply feared for his life because the pharaoh had ordered to have Hebrew newborns killed, but because God had instructed her of what to do to protect this messenger of God and because he promised to return the child to her. And that is what happens in both the Jewish Torah and the Qur'an. Moses (pbuh) was accepted into the pharaoh's household, but Moses' (pbuh) mother was chosen to wean him.

His Mishap

In the Jewish Torah, we read of Moses (pbuh), as an adult at this point, witnessing an altercation between a Hebrew and an Egyptian (Ex. 2:11). Moses (pbuh) is depicted as a person who has capitalized on an opportunity to commit a crime and conceal it. It appears that Moses (pbuh) has malicious intentions in the Jewish Torah.

Exodus 2:12 And he looked this way and that way, and when he saw that there was no man, he smote the Egyptian, and hid him in the sand.

Noticeably, in the Qur'an the men are not called "Hebrews" and "Egyptians." The two are referred to as "one of his party" and "his enemy" (Al-Qur'an 28:15). This narrative avoids the perception that Moses (pbuh) is racial motivated. The title "one of his party" denotes that this person shares in the belief system that Moses' (pbuh) has, thus "his enemy" is someone in opposition to that belief (The fact that several Hebrews rejected Moses' (pbuh) message and many Egyptians risked death for accepting his message in the Qur'an makes it more reasonable to use the terms given here). And in the Qur'an, Moses (pbuh) stumbles upon this fight and the "man of his party" asked Moses (pbuh) for help. Apparently, this man is being beaten by the other man, so he begs to be rescued. At which point Moses (pbuh) strikes the man with his fist and kills "his enemy." Now what do we expect a man appointed by God to do in this situation? Hide the body and run as he does in the Jewish Torah?

Al-Qur'an 28:15 He said: "This is a work of Evil (Satan): for he is an enemy that manifestly misleads!"
Al-Qur'an 28:16 He prayed: "O my Lord! I have indeed wronged my soul! Do Thou then forgive me!" So (Allah) forgave him: for He is the Oft-Forgiving, Most Merciful.

In the Qur'an, Moses (pbuh) realizes that the "man of his party" was actually in the wrong and he immediately asked for God's forgiveness.

And it was granted to him. None of this is mentioned in the Jewish Torah. But can any sensible person deny that the Qur'anic narration of repentance and forgiveness is more suitable for a messenger of God, than the claim in the Jewish Torah that Moses (pbuh) merely "hid him in the sand?" Despite God's forgiveness for Moses' (pbuh) sincere repentance, Moses (pbuh) is again led to help this same man of his party from "an enemy of them both" in another altercation the next day. However that man described as (both of) their enemy makes mention of the Moses' (pbuh) murder and Moses (pbuh) flees for his life.

This story typifies the view of prophets in the Jewish Torah. Moses (pbuh) is perhaps the greatest figure and hero of the entire Hebrew Scripture, yet he is painted as a cold-blooded murderer. This is not the only incident in which the Jewish Torah depicts him as such. He is ruthless in his pursuit of the Promised Land. He leaves no prisoners of war, aside from virgin girls. Islam is ridiculed for those Muslims who commit suicide with the promise of 72 virgins in heaven. If you read the Quran upside down and backwards, you will not find this promise. This claim is to be found in Hadiths, which are supposed to be the words and deeds of Prophet Muhammad (pbuh). And all Muslims accept that some Hadiths are of questionable reliability and are suggest to analysis and scrutiny from a historic and most importantly Quranic standpoint. Criticizing Islam of the basis of such Hadiths could be equated to the criticism of Judaism on the basis of the Talmud, which contains very provocation material. The book of ultimate authority for Jews is the Jewish Torah and the Jewish Torah records Moses (pbuh) kidnaping thousands of virgins in this life. More distasteful is God's participation in this kind of activity by way of his priest, Eleazar. Interestingly 32 virgins are to be dedicated to God. Perhaps this is no coincidence. Perhaps the author of the Hadiths got his idea from the Bible. (More examples of this is in my book entitled "Islam Is The Truth")

Moses (pbuh) is said to have trespassed against God (Deut. 32:4852). He is also told not to touch the land of the Ammonites (Deut. 2:17-19,37), though it is not recorded in the Jewish Torah, we find in the continuation of the children of Israel's story from Joshua that Moses (pbuh) gave the Ammonites' land away (Joshua 13:2425). This kind of behavior is in sharp contrast to the Moses (pbuh) of the Qur'an, who is quick to seek God's guidance, and even before prophethood, he is heedful of God and he is very repentant. This is a man who God entrusted with the moral and legal code for his worshippers to live by. Would you abide by the laws given to you by a man who is incapable of following them himself? I would ask, which Moses (pbuh) would be the better example to follow, the Moses (pbuh) of the Qur'an or that of the Jewish Torah? In the same vein, of all the men chosen to receive revelation and inspiration from God, which includes Adam, Abraham, Jacob or Noah (pbut), which are more of a role model for their followers, the Qur'anic or Jewish Torahic figures?

His Call

The Jewish Torah says Moses (pbuh) was tending to his father-inlaw's flock when he saw a burning bush. The Qur'an says Moses (pbuh) was traveling with his family, when he perceived a fire. In the Qur'an, God instantaneously identifies himself.

Al-Quran 20:14 "Verily, I am Allah: There is no god but I."

There is no ambiguity about these statements at all, which is what we are more likely to expect from God. Chapter 27 and 28 adds that God says to Moses (pbuh) that he is "the exalted in might, the wise" and "Lord of the worlds." So we have "Verily I am Allah, the exalted in might, the wise, Lord of the Worlds. There is no God but I." Compare this with the answer the Jewish Torah claims God spoke in order to identify himself (Ex. 3:14-16 & 6:2-3)

Exodus 3:14 And G-d said unto Moses: 'I AM THAT I AM'; and He said: 'Thus shalt thou say unto the children of Israel: I AM hath sent me unto you.'

Exodus 3:15 And G-d said moreover unto Moses: 'Thus shalt thou say unto the children of Israel: HaShem, the G-d of your fathers, the G-d of Abraham, the G-d of Isaac, and the G-d of Jacob, hath sent me unto you; this is My name for ever, and this is My memorial unto all generations.
Exodus 3:16 Go, and gather the elders of Israel together, and say unto them: HaShem, the G-d of your fathers, the G-d of Abraham, of Isaac, and of Jacob, hath appeared unto me, saying: I have surely remembered you, and seen that which is done to you in Egypt.
Exodus 6:2 And G-d spoke unto Moses, and said unto him: 'I am HaShem;
Exodus 6:3 and I appeared unto Abraham, unto Isaac, and unto Jacob, as G-d Almighty, but by My name I made Me not known to them.

In the Jewish Torah, we find Moses (pbuh) reluctant to carry God's message due to his speech impediment. He must be informed by God, of the powers of God to heal his impediment. At which point, Moses (pbuh) still shows reluctance. Moses' (pbuh) stubbornness, disbelief and fear "kindles God's anger." So, God appoints Aaron, Moses' brother as his mouthpiece and Moses now takes the place of god to Aaron (pbut) (Ex. 4:16). In the Qur'an, Moses (pbuh) is apprehensive. When he first witnesses the rod turn into a snake, he runs away in fear (Al-Qur'an 27:10). This is a normal reaction. When he settles down, he is given instructions. Upon receiving his orders, the Qur'an quotes Moses (pbuh) as saying the following:

Al-Qur'an 20:25 (Moses) said: "O my Lord! expand me my breast;
Al-Qur'an 20:26 "Ease my task for me;
Al-Qur'an 20:27 "And remove the impediment from my speech,
Al-Qur'an 20:28 "So they may understand what I say:
Al-Qur'an 20:29 "And give me a Minister from my family,
Al-Qur'an 20:30 "Aaron, my brother;
Al-Qur'an 20:31 "Add to my strength through him,
Al-Qur'an 20:32 "And let him share my task

It is abundantly clear that Moses (pbuh) knows the power of God and he asks God for tools to help him succeed. And God is not upset with Moses, nor does he make Moses a god to Aaron (pbut). Aaron is not even a mouthpiece to Moses (pbut) but a fellow minister and a prophet of God. God heals Moses (pbuh) of his affliction in the Qur'an and he grants Moses' (pbuh) wishes. But if we read further, we find that God tells Moses (pbuh) that he has guided Moses (pbuh) since his birth and throughout his life (Al-Qur'an 20: 37-41). So God is emphasizing that he was always on this path to prophethood and so too was every prophet of God, including his brother, Aaron (pbuh).

The Pharaoh

In the Qur'an as in the Jewish Torah, the pharaoh had enslaved the children of Israel. God commands Moses and his brother, Aaron (pbut) to tell the pharaoh to free them from slavery. Unlike the Jewish Torah, the Qur'an maintains that Moses (pbuh) was not only interested in freeing the Israelites but also in converting the pharaoh and the Egyptians to his beliefs in the one true God. The Egyptians were worshipping the pharaoh as God (Al-Qur'an 26:29). God instructs Moses (pbuh) to speak to the pharaoh "mildly perchance he may take warning or fear (Allah)" (Al-Qur'an 20:44). The pharaoh and his chiefs ridiculed Moses and Aaron (pbut) for attempting to convert them from their beliefs handed down from their forefathers (Al-Qur'an 10:78). This is a very important aspect of Moses' (pbuh) message. In the Qur'an, he is not only worried about the well-being of the Israelites, but of all the people he encounters, even his enemies. As a messenger of God, he is obligated to offer God's truth to everyone. This need or want to convert anyone is conspicuously absent in the Jewish Torah. The understanding from the Qur'an is that God's people are all those who accept his message.

Despite Moses' (pbuh) explanation and signs of the one true God, the pharaoh's arrogance drove him to disbelief. However, not every Egyptian was so arrogant. In the Qur'an, the pharaoh fears the conversion of his people (Al-Qur'an 40:26) and for good reason. The magician, who attempted to rival Moses' (pbuh) miracle, and many countryman converted to Moses' (pbuh) beliefs. And they were even persecuted for their conversion, but they behaved as martyrs for their newfound faith (Al-Qur'an 26:46-51, 40:28-46). According to the Qur'an, even the pharaoh's wife became a believer (Al-Quran 66:11). At the pharaoh's final hour, before being consumed by the waters split by God for Moses' (pbuh) escape, he too bore witness to the one true God.

I am not insinuating that because these aspects of the story of Moses (pbuh) are in the Qur'an, they should be believed. I am insinuating that their inclusion is reasonable and logical and that it makes more sense than their exclusion. It is more reasonable to believe that a prophet of God sought guidance for others and that those who witnessed his miracles came into his fold. The Qur'anic version includes information not found in the Jewish Torah and it excludes a major portion of the Jewish Torah's account of Moses (pbuh) and the pharaoh.

The Qur'an declares that God gave Moses (pbuh) nine signs to demonstrate his power, in hopes of converting the pharaoh (Al-Quran 7:130-132). Yet the Jewish Torah illustrates ten signs given to Moses (pbuh). The tenth sign being the death of every firstborn Egyptian child (Ex. 11:4-5). Does the Qur'an's exclusion of God killing every Egyptians firstborn give more credibility to the Qur'an or the Jewish Torah?

The Golden Calf

Aaron (pbuh) in the Qur'an is regarded as a prophet of God. He assisted his brother in his mission of freeing the children of Israel from the pharaoh. As someone who delivers God's message to mankind, this person is quite naturally held in high regard as a man of honor, truth and righteousness. The Qur'an exonerates Aaron (pbuh) from the accusation that he made the golden calf for the Israelites to worship. Considering his esteemed position with God and his experiences with God's power in both the Qur'an and the Jewish Torah, any reader should find it peculiar that such a man would violate the first and most important commandment of God, that being to carve an image and worship it besides his "jealous" God.

The Qur'an substantiates any apprehension one might have in this regard. Aaron was placed in charge of the people while Moses (pbut) was receiving revelations from God (Al-Qur'an 7:142). The Qur'an does not give the precise name of the culprit, but it identifies the man responsible for the Israelites worshipping the golden calf to be As-Samiri. *{There have been some issues raised about the Qur'an's use of the title "As-Samiri." The title has been understood to be the Arabic word for the Samaritan. It has been alleged that Samaritans were not established as a nation at the time of Moses, therefore any reference to them at the time of Moses would be an anachronism.*

"Referring to the Bible we can note two interesting facts. First let's refer to Ezekiel: "The word of the LORD came to me: "Son of man, confront Jerusalem with her detestable practices and say, 'This is what the Sovereign LORD says to Jerusalem: Your ancestry and birth were in the land of the Canaanites; your father was an Amorite and your mother a Hittite. [Bible, Ezekiel 16:1-3]

The chapter continues making much use of metaphorical language to describe Jerusalem and it's adulterous practices until we reach the following: "You (Jerusalem) are a true daughter of your mother, who despised her husband and her children; and you are a true sister of your sisters, who despised their husbands and their children. Your mother was a Hittite and your father an Amorite. Your older sister was Samaria,..." [Bible, Ezekiel 16:45,46]

According to this chapter Samaria is the older sister of Jerusalem. Does the Bible then not recognize the antiquity of Samaria?-http://www.answering-christianity.com/quran/svirk.htm

Jerusalem existed in the time of Abraham (Gen. 14:18), yet Samaria or the land of the Samaritans is said to be older that Jerusalem. Therefore it is not an anachronism at all, to call a man at the time of Moses "As-Samiri".}

The Qur'an says this man formed the golden calf and many of the Israelites worshipped it. As a prophet of God, Aaron (pbuh) is obliged to denounce such acts. But some of the Israelites were hell-bent on this form of worship and they threatened to kill Aaron (pbuh), if he intervened (Al-Qur'an 7:150). Thus fearing repercussions and division amongst the children of Israel, Aaron awaited Moses' (pbut) return (Al-Qur'an 20:94). The Qur'an also records that many of the Israelites came to their senses and repented, even before Moses (pbuh) returned (Al-Qur'an 7:149).

When God tells him of this people's transgressions, Moses (pbuh) is infuriated. This is in contrast to the Jewish Torah, which asserts that God was incensed by their sin. The Qur'an again and again tells its reader about the sinner that "to us (God) they did no harm, but they harmed their own souls (Al-Qur'an 2:57). However Moses (pbuh) was enraged by the Israelite's sin. In haste, he grabs Aaron (pbuh) and accuses him of allowing his people to worship the calf. As a great example for his people, Moses upon hearing Aaron's explanation immediately repented to God for his rush to judgment about Aaron's (pbut) inability to halt the sins of the people (Al-Qur'an 7:151). Moses (pbuh) exiled As-Samiri for his mischief (Al-Qur'an 20:97). Those who begged for God's forgiveness, God granted it to them (Al- Qur'an 2:52). The Qur'an does affirm what the Jewish Torah states that the Israelites slew the guilty. But the guilty, in the Qur'an, are those who received clear guidance from God, went astray and did not repent and most importantly sought to kill a messenger of God. So apostasy was not the cause for their death, but attempted murder was.

Another slight difference in the Qur'an is that Moses (pbuh) demonstrated the helplessness of the golden calf by burning it and casting its ashes into the sea (Al-Qur'an 20:97), whereas the Jewish Torah has the Israelites drinking the golden calf when it is grained into powder. The Jewish Torah would have the reader believe that Moses diffused God's anger and kindled his wrath. The Qur'an mentions Moses (pbuh) appealing, not counseling, to God not to destroy him and his people by way of an earthquake. It is obvious that this is an appeal because Moses (pbuh) acknowledges the situation to be a "trial." So the earthquake was a warning to the Israelite people. To assure Moses (pbuh) and the reader who is actually in charge, God says "With My punishment I visit whom I will, but My mercy extendeth to all things" (Al-Qur'an 7:155-156). In the Qur'an, God needs no counsel or direction at anytime. In other words, Moses' (pbuh) words had no bearing on the punishment or mercy which ALLAH decrees for them.

Moses' (pbuh) Request

In the Jewish Torah, there is the account of Moses (pbuh) asking to see God (Exodus 33:18). In response, God said that his "goodness" will pass by Moses (pbuh), but Moses (pbuh) will not see God's face. God says no man can see him and live. At this point, God places Moses (pbuh) in the cleft of a rock, God places his hand over the cleft and passes by Moses (pbuh).

Exodus 33:23 And I will take away My hand, and thou shalt see My back: but My face shall not be seen.

The Qur'an recounts the same request of Moses (pbuh) to God, but the events after the request are different.

Al-Qur'an 7:143 When Moses came to the place appointed by Us, and his Lord addressed him, He said: "O my Lord! show (Thyself) to me, that I may look upon thee." Allah said: "By no means canst thou see Me (direct); But look upon the mount; if it abide in its place, then shalt thou see Me." When his

Lord manifested His glory on the Mount, He made it as dust. And Moses fell down in a swoon. When he recovered his senses he said: "Glory be to Thee! to Thee I turn in repentance, and I am the first to believe."

The Jewish Torah gives the impression that God's hand and back are accessible to the human eye. It is his face that cannot be seen by man. The Qur'an makes no such distinguish. In fact, it makes no mention of literal body parts of God. The Qur'an asserts that merely his revealed glory can crumble a mountain. The sight of the crumbled mountain alone quenches Moses' (pbuh) thirst to see God. It is left a mystery in the Jewish Torah, whether or not God's hand and back were sufficient for Moses (pbuh). I would suggest that these two stories juxtaposed present a clear case for the Qur'anic view that it is not a copy but a correction of the Jewish Torah we have today. The Qur'an asserts that no man can see God and this premise is consistent throughout. The Jewish Torah on a couple of occasions suggests that no man can see God and live (Gen. 32:30, Ex. 33:20), but on even more occasions demonstrate that God had been seen without repercussion (Gen. 12:7, 17:1, 18:1, 26:2, 26:24, 32:30 35:9, 48:3, Ex. 3:16, 4:5, 6:3, 33:11, 33:23, Deut. 5:4). It may be possible to understand a few of these instances to be figurative, but it is difficult to figuratively understand seeing God face to face, and eating, drinking and interacting with him.

THE GOD OF THE QUR'AN AND THE GOD OF THE JEWISH TORAH

Both books are adamant about the worship of the one true God. They both agree that there are not to be any graven images of God. However they differ on the reasoning behind this law. First, the Jewish Torah is filled with images of God. When reading the Jewish Torah you are almost forced to draw a picture in your mind of God, given all his humanistic characteristics. You have God making people in his image, people are hiding from God, people see his face, hand and back, he comes down to earth on occasion, he eats food and he is grappled with. It is practically impossible to think of him as anything other than a man. Also he is not explicitly called a spiritual or immaterial being. This is perhaps the reason many Christians consider the Jewish Torah's accounts of God to actually be Jesus (pbuh). Given the description of God in the Jewish Torah, it is conceivable that Abraham, Moses or Jacob (pbut) could have actually made a graven image of God since they actually saw him. The Qur'an dispels any idea of an image of God with one verse, "there is nothing comparable to him" (Al-Qur'an 112:4). Therefore making a graven image of him is impossible and any attempt to would automatically be limiting and lowering God to your complete imagination.

The Jewish Torah says that God does not want his followers to have any other gods because God is jealous, but jealous of whom? Apparently God is jealous of the other god, if you worship it. This means that God's praise is REQUIRED to appease him and fulfill his needs. Quite the opposite is true in the Qur'an, the servant is in need of praising God.

The first verse of the Qur'an begins "*Alhamdulillah*" which means "all praise is DUE to God." He does not need our praise, but he deserves our praise. The Qur'an says God fulfills the needs of his creation, but he needs nothing. He is self-subsisting (Al-Qur'an 2:255). Praise and remembrance of God is beneficial to us and our souls, not to God. It brings us closer to him. Also, your rejection of God to worship other gods or to worship nothing at all will not harm him in the least. Sin will harm you and your soul (Al- Qur'an 2:57). He has no need to be jealous. The Qur'an takes the position that belief in the one true God will lead you on the right path, but belief in other than the one true God will lead you astray, because if you are following the wrong leader you will ultimately be led on the wrong path. To put it in more applicable terms, if you are in America, yet you recognize and adhere to the laws of China, it is inevitable that you will offend the laws of America. So the Qur'an's stance on the oneness of God and its adherence has nothing to do with God's jealousy and everything to do with man's position on the straight path.

Besides God's jealousy, God is quite angry in the Jewish Torah. At first glance it appears that God's anger is actually a personification of his wrath for punishment. Punishment denotes justice, while anger implies an emotion which should be excluded from God's characteristics. Anger might cause an individual to make a rash discussion, like "wiping man off the face of the earth." The fact that the Jewish Torah records God considering this option for the sins of a certain group of people gives validity to the understanding that God's anger in the Jewish Torah was not metaphorical, but literal. Because of the sins of Israel, God is said to have regretted making mankind and he contemplated getting rid of everybody. Moses' (pbuh) advice and God's reconsideration give further weight to the notion that God is upset by the actions of his people. The Qur'an says you harm yourself, not God. But this is not to say that God does not have affection for his creation. He is both just (Al-Qur'an 95:8) and loving (Al-Qur'an 11:90) to his creation, but he is not enraged by their actions. Also if God is forgiving and merciful to the children of Israel, then he must be this way for everyone.

LAWS

Tax

The Jewish Torah mentions a tax on the rich and the poor for their atonement, in which the amount is equal for both parties (Exodus 30:11-16). Islam however garners a charity or Zakat which is for the poor, the homeless, orphans and others in need. Even more reasonable is that this amount is base on a percentage of a person's earnings, not a fixed amount. This regulation takes into account the value of each person's contribution. The charity of $50 can be equivalent to that of a wealthy man's $100,000. Something else quite significant is that atonement is not gained monetarily in Islam, but through sincere repentance and if possible retribution (Al-Qur'an 4:17-18, 39:53-54).

Al-Qur'an 9:60 Alms are for the poor and the needy, and those employed to administer the (funds); for those whose hearts have been (recently) reconciled (to Truth); for those in bondage and in debt; in the cause of Allah; and for the wayfarer: (thus is it) ordained by Allah, and Allah is full of knowledge and wisdom.

Zakat is charity for Muslims. However there is a form of tax for non-Muslims in countries governed by Islam, called jizya. This tax is often used by non-Muslims to pronounce some false claim of oppression by the Muslims on those who do not except Islam. To briefly dispel this notion, let us first realize that Zakat is obligatory on Muslims. Would it be oppressive to have non-Muslims pay some form of tax, as well? I have worked my entire adult life and I have never paid taxes. The government takes the tax out of my check. Before I get paid, the taxes are paid. These taxes, like jizya, are to provide for the welfare of those in need. Is this practice oppressive? Furthermore, the jizya is less than the Zakat that a Muslims pays.

Unsolved Murder

The Qur'an, on several occasions, deals with similar issues mentioned in the Jewish Torah and it invites Jews and Christians (calling them "People of the Book") to consider the alternative to many of their beliefs and doctrines. This may be due to the fact that Jews, Christians and Muslims share so many beliefs from the onset, that it is a much easier transition for them to Islam, if they found the Qur'an to be more accurate on the issues that it addresses. It should be stated that the Qur'an does not go down a list and say "this is wrong" and "this is wrong." The Qur'an simply states "this is right" and if you doubt it, research it further and then decide. So the Qur'an calls for an investigation into the truth, with the notion that an investigation for a Jew, Christian or a skeptic will convinced them of the Qur'an's validity. For Muslims, who are already convinces, it will strengthen this conviction.

An unsolved murder in the Israelite community is an issue which the Jewish Torah and the Qur'an address. The Jewish Torah demands that the elders of the city must get a young female cow, and kill it. At which point, a priest will bless the cow and the elders will wash their hands over the animal.

Deuteronomy 21:7-8 "And they shall speak and say: 'Our hands have not shed this blood, neither have our eyes seen it. Forgive, O HaShem, Thy people Israel, whom Thou hast redeemed, and suffer not innocent blood to remain in the midst of Thy people Israel.' And the blood shall be forgiven them"

The details of this law demonstrate that God holds the community responsible for an unsolved murder. Therefore the elders must perform this ritual to gain everyone's forgiveness. This law is important for Christians as well as Jews, because in this law we begin to see how blood of the innocent sacrifice can bring forth forgiveness in the scriptures held sacred by both groups.

The Qur'an, on the other hand, does not record this ritual as a commandment to be followed in the future at all. And it asserts that the blood of this animal is not for anyone's forgiveness. Nor does the Qur'an suggest that the community is to blame for an unsolved murder. What the Qur'an does describe is a particular incident in which a man was slain and there were no witnesses amongst the children of Israel. God had Moses (pbuh) have the Israelites to kill an unblemished female cow.

Al-Qur'an 2:72 Remember ye slew a man and fell into a dispute among yourselves as to the crime: But Allah was to bring forth what ye did hide.
Al-Qur'an 2:73 So We said: "Strike the (body) with a piece of the (heifer)." Thus Allah bringeth the dead to life and showeth you His Signs: Perchance ye may understand.

The Qur'an says that the cow was not for the people's forgiveness, but an instrument used to perform a miracle. This miracle was to bring the "dead to life" so he could show who his killer was. The account in the Qur'an essentially says that "God is aware of the guilty party, even if you are not." This is in contrast to the Jewish Torah, which presents a supposed law of God in which he holds everyone responsible, as if he is unaware who the perpetrator is.

Slavery

One of the most puzzling aspects of the Jewish Torah is the hypocrisy of some of its laws. Injustices perpetuated against the Israelites are condemned by God, yet the very same injustices performed by the Israelites are condoned by God, with slavery being a glaring example. The enslavement of the children of Israel was so unjust that it called for God's intervention through Moses and Aaron (pbut). Yet, later we read that Moses established laws which empowered his people to make slaves of others and from among themselves. Of course, the Hebrew slave is eligible to leave after 6 years (Ex. 21:2), whereas the foreign slave may serve indefinitely. These slaves are considered to be property.

Leviticus 25:44 And as for thy bondmen, and thy bondmaids, whom thou mayest have: of the nations that are round about you, of them shall ye buy bondmen and bondmaids.
Leviticus 25:45 Moreover of the children of the strangers that do sojourn among you, of them may ye buy, and of their families that are with you, which they have begotten in your land; and they may be your possession.
Leviticus 25:46 And ye may make them an inheritance for your children after you, to hold for a possession: of them may ye take

your bondmen for ever; but over your brethren the children of Israel ye shall not rule, one over another, with rigour.

This is basically slavery in a nutshell in the Jewish Torah. The slave's wife and children are also property of his master (Ex. 21:34). A slave's freedom comes from marriage (Deut. 20:10-13) or if the master injuries the slave's eye or tooth (Ex. 21:26-27). It should be noted that the laws of the Jewish Torah pertaining to slavery are seldom practiced in this day and time, but this does not explain their presence in the first place nor does it alleviate the possibility for their adherence at a later date if one beliefs them to be the laws of God.

Slavery was definitely present and a force to be reckoned with in the time of Prophet Muhammad (pbuh) and many Muslims played major roles in the slave trades throughout history. The question is not about the actions of Muslims, but what are the commandments to Muslims? When slaves are spoken of in the Qur'an they are called "those who your right hand possess." This is because the Qur'an is speaking of prisoners of war, not kidnapped people.

The Qur'an like the Jewish Torah encourages marriage of a slave, but of a "BELIEVING" slave (Al-Qur'an 4:25). It has been alleged that the Qur'an allows Muslims to fornicate with slave women because of these verses:

Al-Qur'an 23:5-6 "And who guard their modesty, save from their wives or the (slaves) that their right hands possess, for then they are not blameworthy.

However this is a common mistake made by opponents of the Qur'an. They read one verse without consideration for other verses which are used together to establish laws. For example, the Qur'an speaks about prayer on several occasions. It makes mention of some of the times of prayer in some verses. An overzealous reader may mistakenly assume that Muslims are only to pray two or three times a day, if they do not consider all the times defined in the Qur'an as prayer time. In relation to the topic of slavery and marriage chapter 24:32 of the Qur'an says a Muslim can marry a slave. Upon reading this verse, one might assume that a Muslim can marry any slave, but chapter 4:25 explains that this must be a "BELIEVING" slave. When you read these two verses in conjunction with 23:5-6, it is incorrect to state that the Qur'an allows Muslims to fornicate with slaves, but that the Qur'an allows relations with a believing freed slave in the sanctity of marriage.

In contrast to the Jewish Torah, the Qur'an never encourages, establishes or endorses slavery. In fact, the Qur'an on several occasions encourages, establishes and endorses the abolition of slavery, without the consideration of a slave's injury. The Qur'an systematically prepared an end to slavery, which is exactly the reason why slavery ended in Arabia. In this case, it is fitting to let the Qur'an speak for itself.

Al-Qur'an 4:36 ...do good- to what your right hands possess

Al-Qur'an 9:60 Alms are ...for those in bondage

Al-Qur'an 4:92 Never should a believer kill a believer; but by mistake, If one (so) kills a believer, it is ordained that he should free a believing slave

Al-Qur'an 5:89 He will call you to account for your deliberate oaths: for expiation give a slave his freedom.

Al-Qur'an 3:79 It is not (possible) for any human being unto whom Allah had given the Scripture and wisdom and the prophethood that he should afterwards have said unto mankind: Be slaves of me instead of Allah's

Al-Qur'an 47:4 So when you meet in battle those who disbelieve, then smite the necks until when you have overcome them, then make (them) prisoners, and afterwards either set them free as a favor or let them ransom (themselves) until the war terminates

Al-Qur'an 2:177 ... it is righteousness... to spend of your substance... for the ransom of slaves

Al-Qur'an 24:33 Let those who find not the wherewithal for marriage keep themselves chaste, until Allah gives them means out of His grace. And if any of your slaves ask for a deed in writing (to enable them to earn their freedom for a certain sum), give them such a deed if ye know any good in them: yea, give them something yourselves out of the means which Allah has given to you.

Suspicion of Ill-conduct

In the Deuteronomy 22:13-21, we read about a husband's claim that his wife is unchaste and the methods used to determine the woman's chastity. This is a truly humiliating method in a public forum to prove a woman's virginity. The woman and her father are response for providing the proof. The Qur'an holds the chastity and honor of women in great regard. Words again fail me in an effort to simulate the seriousness of this charge in the Qur'an.

Al-Qur'an 24:4 And those who launch a charge against chaste women, and produce not four witnesses (to support their allegations),- flog them with eighty stripes; and reject their evidence ever after: for such men are wicked transgressors;
Al-Qur'an 24:5 Unless they repent thereafter and mend (their conduct); for Allah is Oft-Forgiving, Most Merciful.
Al-Qur'an 24:6 And for those who launch a charge against their spouses, and have (in support) no evidence but their own,- their solitary evidence (can be received) if they bear witness four times (with an oath) by Allah that they are solemnly telling the truth;
Al-Qur'an 24:7 And the fifth (oath) (should be) that they solemnly invoke the curse of Allah on themselves if they tell a lie.
Al-Qur'an 24:8 But it would avert the punishment from the wife, if she bears witness four times (with an oath) By Allah, that (her husband) is telling a lie;
Al-Qur'an 24:9 And the fifth (oath) should be that she solemnly invokes the wrath of Allah on herself if (her accuser) is telling the truth.
Al-Qur'an 24:10 If it were not for Allah's grace and mercy on you, and that Allah is Oft-Returning, full of Wisdom,- (Ye would be ruined indeed).
Al-Qur'an 24:11 Those who brought forward the lie are a body among yourselves: think it not to be an evil to you; On the contrary it is good for you: to every man among them (will come the punishment) of the sin that he earned, and to him who took on himself the lead among them, will be a penalty grievous.

Al-Qur'an 24:12 Why did not the believers - men and women - when ye heard of the affair,- put the best construction on it in their own minds and say, "This (charge) is an obvious lie"?
Al-Qur'an 24:13 Why did they not bring four witnesses to prove it? When they have not brought the witnesses, such men, in the sight of Allah, (stand forth) themselves as liars!
Al-Qur'an 24:14 Were it not for the grace and mercy of Allah on you, in this world and the Hereafter, a grievous penalty would have seized you in that ye rushed glibly into this affair.
Al-Qur'an 24:15 Behold, ye received it on your tongues, and said out of your mouths things of which ye had no knowledge; and ye thought it to be a light matter, while it was most serious in the sight of Allah.
Al-Qur'an 24:16 And why did ye not, when ye heard it, say? - "It is not right of us to speak of this: Glory to Allah! this is a most serious slander!"
Al-Qur'an 24:17 Allah doth admonish you, that ye may never repeat such (conduct), if ye are (true) Believers.
Al-Qur'an 24:18 And Allah makes the Signs plain to you: for Allah is full of knowledge and wisdom.
Al-Qur'an 24:19 Those who love (to see) scandal published broadcast among the Believers, will have a grievous Penalty in this life and in the Hereafter: Allah knows, and ye know not.
Al-Qur'an 24:20 Were it not for the grace and mercy of Allah on you, and that Allah is full of kindness and mercy, (ye would be ruined indeed).
Al-Qur'an 24:21 O ye who believe! follow not Satan's footsteps: if any will follow the footsteps of Satan, he will (but) command

what is shameful and wrong: and were it not for the grace and mercy of Allah on you, not one of you would ever have been pure: but Allah doth purify whom He pleases: and Allah is One Who hears and knows (all things).

I can only add this question, would you prefer the system in which the woman, accused of being unchaste, and her family have to prove her innocence or the system in which the accuser has to prove his accusations or face punishment himself?

The Disabled Believer

The Jewish Torah asserts that God says the presence of a disabled person, whether he is blind, lame or maimed, a dwarf, etc is a profanity to God's holy places (Lev. 21:16-23). The Qur'an makes no such distinction against those afflicted with illnesses.

Al-Qur'an 9:18 The mosques of Allah shall be visited and maintained by such as believe in Allah and the Last Day, establish regular prayers, and practice regular charity, and fear none (at all) except Allah.

Which Book is preferable in this instance? Is not the Qur'an's stance a just and moral one? Is not the Qur'anic stance a correction of the Jewish Torah's?

Apostasy and Religious Tolerance

I have cited several laws of the Jewish Torah which pronounce death upon those who turn away from the beliefs of the Jewish Torah (Ex.22:20, 32:27-28, Deut. 17:2-7). Death is also prescribed for your friends or family members who suggest a different faith to you (Deut. 13:6-10). The laws of the Jewish Torah also lack tolerance for other religions (Ex. 22:18, Ex. 23:24, 34:11-14, Deut. 12:2-3).

Try as you like, but you will never find a verse in the Qur'an which authorizes the killing of a person simply because he is of another faith or of no faith, nor will you find a verse enabling Muslims to kill those who have turned from Islam. The Qur'an maintains that this is a matter left up to God to solve.

Al-Qur'an 4:137 Those who believe, then reject faith, then believe (again) and (again) reject faith, and go on increasing in unbelief,Allah will not forgive them nor guide them nor guide them on the way.

Al-Qur'an 47:34 Those who reject Allah, and hinder (men) from the Path of Allah, then die rejecting Allah,- Allah will not forgive them.

These two verses of the Qur'an solidify the claim that the Qur'an leaves the affairs of other's beliefs to God. A person can reject and accept Islam as many times as he likes. A person can even hinder others from the true path in words (not by force) and still God is the judge of this matter.

The Hand

The Jewish Torah and the Qur'an have something in common as it pertains to punishment, which I found interesting. Both of them use the cutting off of a criminal's hand as a form of punishment. However the crimes for this punishment are very different. In the Qur'an, this punishment is for thievery or robbery (Al-Qur'an 5:38), whereas the Jewish Torah gives this punishment to a women who has grabbed the private parts of a man to disengage him in a fight with her husband (Deut. 25:11- 12).

Crimes, related to theft and robbery of any kind, are scourges on society. Not only do these crimes affect the victim, but due to measures taken for compensation for stolen property and prevention of these crimes, they affect every law abiding tax payer. Of course, there are degrees of theft and reasons for theft which are taken into consideration before such a severe punishment is performed. And since the Qur'an prescribed laws which are not only to punish, but to completely discourage anyone from committing the same offense, it is noteworthy that when this punishment is instituted into the laws of a country, this crime is virtually non-existent. There is no criminal and no victim. The punishment becomes the prevention, and compensation is not necessary.

On the other hand, the law mentioned in the Jewish Torah, even if we were to take out the physical altercation between the two men, regulates an offense that is not prevalent in any society that I am aware of. It is an action that is used in a time of desperation, therefore it is most likely a form of defense and it probably should not be punishable at all. Anything other than self-defense or defense of someone else would render this action a sexual offense, which is in no way implied in this law. Therefore, I feel the Jewish Torah gives this punishment as a form of humiliation for a woman who is protecting a loved one, and the Qur'an's punishment is to eliminate a plague on society, which has proven effective. Could the Jewish Torah's law positively affect anyone's life?

The Qur'an and the Holy Land

Al-Qur'an 7:137 And We made a people, considered weak (and of no account), inheritors of lands in both east and west, - lands whereon We sent down Our blessings. The fair promise of thy Lord was fulfilled for the Children of Israel, because they had patience and constancy, and We leveled to the ground the great works and fine buildings which Pharaoh and his people erected (with such pride).

The Promised Land for the Children of Israel is mentioned in the Qur'an, probably to the disbelief of many. The Qur'an in chapter 5:21-26 calls it the "holy" land. Many people are under the assumption that Abraham (pbuh) did not receive the promise, only his offspring. The Jewish Torah says that God promised Abraham (pbuh) the land (Gen. 12:7) and it explicitly states that he dwelled there (Gen. 13:12) and he bought some land of Canaan from the Hittites for his wife, Sarah (Gen. 23:19-20). Yet the Christian's New Testament claims that God did not give Abraham (pbuh) enough Canaanite land to set his foot upon (Acts 7:5). Perhaps the only manner in which God GIVES the Canaanite land is through theft and murder. Actually paying for the property that you desire is not a means by which God GIVES.

The Qur'an also affirms the Jewish Torah's position on the land but it defends the righteous character of Abraham, Lot, Isaac and Jacob (pbut). And it clearly states that Abraham received and possessed the land.

Al-Qur'an 21:71 But We delivered him (Abraham) and (his nephew) Lut (and directed them) to the land which We have blessed for the nations.
Al-Qur'an 21:72 And We bestowed on him Isaac and, as an additional gift, (a grandson), Jacob, and We made righteous men of every one (of them).

The fact that the Children of Israel were returning to their own land after their emancipation from Egypt helps to establish why they were in battle with its inhabitants at that time. The Jewish Torah merely states that the people were sexually immoral and of a different faith, which is not a justifiable reason to take someone's property. The Jewish Torah also accuses the Children of Israel of killing everything in its path to get their land back. Of course, this is not substantiated in the Qur'an.

The terms for the ownership of the land are well document in the Jewish Torah. The Children of Israel are to keep the commandments of God forever and they will have the land forever (Deut. 4:40) and if they do not keep all the laws they will be in a state of torment (Lev. 26:14-33). The Qur'an says that they did not keep God's laws (Al-Quran 2:83-86). The Jewish Torah is filled with details of their transgression of the most important laws. But even more problematic is that those Jews, who wish to return to God's law today, cannot do so with the authority of the Jewish Torah that they possess. It is obvious that it is not the book of God and it is not the book of Moses (pbuh). Though it specifically warns not to add or subtract anything from the laws (Deut. 4:2), it is apparent that this particular law went unheeded. Remember the Israelite prophet Jeremiah attests to this fact (Jer. 8:8). That means that it is seemingly impossible to keep God's law because the Jewish Torah does not contain it.

It is quite possible that those who follow these teachings have not found their long awaited "Messiah" because the books used to identify him are not the words of God. It may be that they have been looking for a man of God using the guidelines from a book of man. The Qur'an asserts that the Messiah has already come as Isa or Jesus (pbuh), son of Mary. Had not the Jews been looking for a person who would lead them to a military victory but an eternal victory, they would have accepted Jesus (pbuh) when he came. In fact, the reason that the Jews of that time had him killed was because he taught about victory in the hereafter and not of military victory. His message along with his miracles was drawing converts. Many of the Jews at that time wanted Jesus (pbuh) to be their king (John 6:15). Caiaphas the high priest convinced some of the Jews that Jesus' (pbuh) mission would ensure that they would never achieve an earthly victory against the Romans. Caiaphas was certain that Jesus' (pbuh) teachings would embolden the Romans to further subjugate the Jews. So Caiaphas said "that it is expedient for us, that one man should die for the people, and that the whole nation perish not (John 11:50). So the pursuit of the land of Israel resulting not only in the rejection of Jesus (pbuh), but also in a death sentence for him.

Many of Jesus' (pbuh) teachings are in opposition to the Jewish Torah, but in total agreement with the teachings of the Qur'an. For instance, Jesus (pbuh) says not to seek worldly gain, but seek God's kingdom, then worldly gain will be given to you (Matt. 6:3133). He said that if you don't pursue the kingdom of heaven, God will substitute you for another people who will (Matt. 21:43). Jesus (pbuh) teaches that the taxes paid by a rich person and a poor should not be viewed the same as the Jewish Torah suggests (Ex. 30:12-15), but the value of their payment is judged by the level of their sacrifice of what they have (Mark 12:41-44). Also interesting is Jesus' (pbuh) words about Lot's (pbuh) wife. While the Jewish Torah says that she merely LOOKED back, Jesus (pbuh) says that she WENT back (Luke 17:31-32), which is in more accordance with the Qur'an.

Jesus (pbuh) also spoke of Jewish Torah without actually endorsing it (John 5:39, 46, 8:17, 10:34). In these verses, Jesus (pbuh) is referring to the Hebrew Scriptures as proof of his prophethood. In essence, he is saying if you read your own scriptures, you would realize that I am the person whom you seek. In the same manner, Prophet Muhammad (pbuh) tells the Jews and Christians, if you read your scriptures, you will see that I am foretold in it. You see, despite the amount of damage done to the scripture, they were unable to totally eradicate the prophecy of Jesus and Muhammad (pbut).

NOW in order for the Jews to be followers of the laws of God, they must come to his final messenger, whom he has bestowed the final revelation and final system of law. The religion of Muhammad (pbuh) is Islam. The Qur'an says this is the religion that every prophet followed. Was Abraham, Isaac, Jacob or Moses (pbut) Jews? Neither of them had even heard the word Jew or Judaism and so they would not be in the habit of telling people to become a Jew or follow Judaism. But they all were of those who were given or adhered to the laws of God. And they would have instructed their followers to adhere to these laws. The Arabic word for acting in accordance with the law or will of God is ISLAM and one who follows his will and laws is a MUSLIM. Therefore Abraham, Moses, Jacob, Isaac (pbut) and all their followers were Muslims, those who submit and do the will of God.

MUSLIMS IN THE JEWISH TORAH

Despite the differences in the Qur'an and the Jewish Torah, the Qur'an says that the Jewish Torah which the Jews and Christians possess does contain some truth. One of these truths is the prophecy of the prophet like Moses (pbuh) and another is described in this verse.

Al-Qur'an 48:29 Muhammad is the apostle of Allah; and those who are with him are strong against Unbelievers, (but) compassionate amongst each other. Thou wilt see them bow and prostrate themselves (in prayer), seeking Grace from Allah and (His) Good Pleasure. On their faces are their marks, (being) the traces of their prostration. This is their similitude in the Taurat (Torah).

In the Jewish Torah, we find out how the prophets prayed.

Genesis 24:52 And it came to pass, that, when Abraham's servant heard their words, he bowed himself down to the earth unto HaShem.

Genesis 17:3 And Abraham fell on his face...
Exodus 34:8 And Moses made haste, and bowed his head toward the earth, and worshipped.

Numbers 16:22 And they (Moses and Aaron) fell upon their faces

Numbers 20:6 And they (Moses and Aaron) fell upon their faces

If one were to look for the form of worship which the Prophets of the Jewish Torah performed, there is no doubt that it has a glaring similitude with the form of worship which 1.8 billion Muslims perform 5 times a day. Even the preparation which Muslims perform before worshipping God is to be found in the Jewish Torah.

Exodus 40:31-32 that Moses and Aaron and his sons might wash their hands and their feet thereat; when they went into the tent of meeting, and when they came near unto the altar, they should wash; as HaShem commanded Moses.

If we venture deeper into the Hebrew and even the Christian Scripture, we find:

Joshua 5:14 And Joshua fell on his face to the earth, and did worship...

1Kings 18:42 And he (Elijah) cast himself down upon the earth, and put his face between his knees.

Matthew 26:39 And he (Jesus) went a little further, and fell on his face, and prayed...

The universal Muslim greeting to one another is *As-Salamu Alaikum*, meaning "Peace be unto you." The words *"Sholom Aleichem"* in Hebrew also means "Peace be with you." And they sound almost identical to the Arabic salutation that all Muslims use. And this greeting is found on the lips of others in the Bible.

Genesis 43:23 (Joseph's steward) But he answered: Peace be with you

Judges 6:23 And HaShem said unto him: 'Peace be unto thee

1Samuel 25:6 (David tells his messengers) ...and thus ye shall say: All hail! and peace be both unto thee

1Chronicles 12:18 (the Spirit of God to David) ...peace, peace be unto thee, and peace be to thy helpers...

Jesus (pbuh) greeted his disciples "Peace to you!" (John 20:19, 20:21, 20:26). It has been said that when a Christian or Jew becomes a Muslims that he has become a better Christian or Jew because he or she more closely follows the examples of the prophets sent by God.

ARAB AND ISRAELI CONFLICT

ISRAEL OR PALESTINE

The word "Canaan" was used by the Egyptians in reference to land that they ruled, which is known to some as Israel and to others as Palestine. It is Israel to the Jews and Palestine to the Arabs who live there. Jews are said to be the descendants of Isaac (pbuh) and Arabs are the descendants of Ishmael (pbuh). I have read on several occasions that the bickering amongst the two groups is a fulfillment of prophecy from the Jewish Torah, where Ishmael was teasing Isaac (pbut). It should be stated that Ishmael was a teenage and Isaac (pbut) was an infant at the time and any quibbling that they may have had is as petty as any other problems between a teen and infant. Not to mention the fact that throughout history, Jews have lived with Muslims in great harmony for centuries. Jews have even lived under Muslim's protection from Christians and others. Is there any prophecy which foretold this? Probably not, but it has become popular for some to perpetuate a conflict between the two and an atmosphere of hopelessness and helplessness. Many people, because they believe that Muslims and Jews are inherent enemies, do nothing to stop the current problems. Even if the conflict raging today was a fulfillment of a prophecy, this does not negate our responsibility to try to resolve the conflict. Some have even made matters worse by dehumanizing the Palestinian and exalting the Jews as heroes. This kind of thinking may be rooted in the Hebrew Scriptures. The Palestinians are the descendants of the Canaanite and Philistines of the Bible and their depiction in Hebrew Scriptures is less than flattering.

DEHUMANIZING THE PALESTINIANS

The Hebrew Scriptures record that a judge named Shamgar singlehandedly killed 600 Philistines with an ox goad (Judge 3:31). An ox goad is a wooden stick used to guide cattle. It is very thin and it ranges from 5 to 10 feet. So, was he helped by angels of God? There is no mention of this. All he had was a stick. This feat is what is done in films and what is told as folklore. Could someone defeat 600 hundred people with a baseball bat? Probably not, let alone a 10 foot thin stick.

The Philistines again fall victim to a mighty man in the Hebrew Scriptures. The legendary Samson killed 1,000 Philistines with the jawbone of a donkey. Again there is no supreme force guiding his hand. An ordinary man killed 1,000 people with a jawbone of a donkey. And he was so elated that he had to sing a song about this feat.

Judge 15:16 And Samson said: With the jawbone of an ass, heaps upon heaps, with the jawbone of an ass have I smitten a thousand men.

Ahmed Deedat, questioning the stories' veracity in one of his lectures, once asked, "When Shamgar and Samson were killing the Philistines, what were the other Philistines doing?" He asked, "Where did Shamgar strike them, to kill them with a stick? You can't kill 600 hundred snowmen with this stick...And if 1,000 Philistines would have spat of Samson, he would have suffocated." Even more incredulous is what Samson did before he killed 1,000 Philistines. He first caught 300 hundred foxes and tied their tails together and set fire to their tails.

Judges 15:5 And when he had set the torches on fire, he let them go into the standing corn of the Philistines, and burnt up both the shocks and the standing corn, and also the oliveyards.

Mr. Deedat asks, "300 foxes in Palestine? Where did he find them? And they all cooperated? Do you know what an ordeal it is to catch one chicken, in the open?" He asked his audience members to try to catch two poodles and tie their tails together. "See what they do to you?"

According to the Jewish Torah, Samson was also the first person in history to use a suicide attack on his enemies. He prayed to God for the strength to crumble a building killing himself and well over 3,000 Philistine men and women. After his prayer, his last words were "'Let me die with the Philistines,' ...so the dead that he slew at this death were more than they that he slew in his life." (Judges 16:26-30) Yet Samson is a celebrated hero in Judaism and in Christianity (Hebrew 11:32-34).

David (pbuh) is attributed with even more inhumane behavior towards the Philistines. As a payment to a king for his daughters hand in marriage, David (pbuh) was to bring back the foreskin of 100 Philistines. David (pbuh) was so "pleased with the idea of being the king's son-in-law, that he goes out and KILLS 200 Philistines and delivers their foreskin to the king (1Sam. 18:27). I shudder to think of how David (pbuh) got those foreskins? In Deuteronomy, it says a woman who grabs the privates of a man must have her hand cut off. Does this same rule not apply in the case of David (pbuh)? He and his men must have violated this law. Yet there is no reprimand from God for this kind of mutilation. The Philistines are seen and treated like something less than human.

Islam again asserts that David (pbuh) was a man of great character and the shameless deeds attributed to him and his son Solomon (pbuh) are nothing more than fiction. Notice the round figures used in these stories, 100, 200, 300, 600, and 1,000. This gives the impression that these are fictional stories. But what do these kinds of stories serve as, other than exaltation of the Israelites and denigration of the Philistine or Palestinian people. What is the effect that such stories might have on people who believe this to be the inspired words of God. If you believe these words to be the words of God, you must view these men of the Bible and their actions as heroic, thus defining their opponents as those in opposition to God. This is the only explanation as to why these stories exist in the scriptures today, with little criticism. When a believer in these scriptures picks up a newspaper and sees the modern day Philistines placed in concentration camps without clean water, without sewage, without medication, without education, without defense, it registers in their minds as a continuation of their punishments of old. They see the Palestinians as less than human. Their condition is not looked at as the atrocity that it is. No other oppressed or underprivileged people on earth are look at as if they deserve the condition that they are in. How does a child 4,000 years removed from Biblical times deserve to be oppressed for what happened in that time?

THE REASON BEHIND THE CONFLICT

To be clear, this is a matter of intolerance of each other's religion, and neither party is fighting to win converts. For a Muslim or a Jew to desist in this battle is to go against their religion. The Jews are fighting Palestinians because they believe God has ordained this land to them at whoever's expense (Fortunately, we have ascertained that this ordinance is proclaimed by someone other than God). And the Muslims are fighting because the Qur'an commands them to fight against those who oppressed them and steal their land. This is self-defense, which is something that is universally accepted. So in essence and in fact, someone's faith must be proven to be inaccurate, in order to solve this conflict with as little bloodshed as possible.

The Palestinians and the Muslims around the world believe that a great injustice has occurred and the Palestinians are the victims. But any sympathizer with the Palestinians is ostracized and marked as an advocate for terrorism and an anti-Semite. Muslims are so preoccupied with establishing their stance against terrorism, that the Palestinians' suffering becomes an afterthought. It should be stated that most of the Palestinians are Muslims, but some are Christians as well. Muslims feel the pain of their brothers and sisters throughout the world. Of course, there are Muslims persecuting others and Muslims being persecuted throughout the world, but no persecution has received more support than the one going on in the Palestine. As Jews galvanized themselves after the atrocities of the Holocaust, so too must the Muslims galvanize ourselves and gain the world's support against occupation and murder. It should go without saying that the act of suicide is an act of desperation. No one wants to win a battle in which they cannot see the victory. People look at every terrorist attack on Israel in terms of "how did this happen?, instead of "why did this happen?" The question "why" in no way justifies suicide bombings, which are totally un-Islamic and un-Qur'anic, but it does help examine the reason for its prevalence.

DEFINE TERRORISM

One reason that the Palestinian struggle is not properly assessed is because most people cannot get beyond this word "terrorism." But the problem lies with the definition of the word "terrorism." If it is left up to the participants of a conflict, they would all call themselves "freedom fighters" and their opponents "terrorists." Though the word "terrorism" is repeated countless times a day, it is very rarely defined. This is because of the implications of its definition.

Terrorism: *the unlawful use or threatened use of force or violence by a person or an organized group against people or property with the intention of intimidating or coercing societies or governments, often for ideological or political reasons.*

Therefore, the culprits of 9/11 and all suicide bombers are terrorists. This definition would also mean that our western powers implored terrorism to gain and expand their territory throughout the world and throughout history. Britain used terrorism to colonize countless countries, including those of North America. Not only was America established on terrorism, but the 13 colonies expanded westward through the use of terrorism. America was built upon the backs of slaves through forced free labor which was terrorism. Lynching, sending attack dogs, spraying water hoses to impose segregation was terrorism. Imposing an ideology on a people who do not want it is terrorism, even if it is democracy. Torture is a form of terrorism.

So too are embargoes and sanctions which restrict food and medicine to a country you are at odds with. These are all acts of violence or threats of violence, not on the military, but on non-combatants or civilians for whatever reason.

President Bush has expanded the definition of terrorism, by saying that anyone who knowingly harbors and/or assists terrorists is to be considered terrorists themselves. The only problem that I see with this expansion is that it implicates its author, who knowingly gave asylum to many known terrorists, like former CIA operative, Luis Posada Carriles. Carriles committed numerous terrorist attacks, including blowing up a Cuban airplane killing 73 people.

If you notice, the definition of terrorism and Bush's expansion of that definition does not give any justification for killing innocent people, because there is none. People imagine in their own minds that some acts of terrorism and some terrorists are acceptable. In 1941, Japanese pilots attacked the United States naval base at Pearl Harbor. They destroyed several of our ships, aircraft and they killed about 2400 people, wounding close to 1200. In response to this despicable surprise attack, which was specifically intended to weaken our military, President Franklin D. Roosevelt executed United States Executive order of 9066 on February 19,1942, which authorized the detainment of 120,000 American, who were of Japanese descent. This order endured until April 19, 1976. 34 years!!! Imprisonment of civilians for the military attacks of others is terrorism. Luckily, in 1983 the Commission on Wartime Relocation and Internment of Civilians (CWRIC), gave the survivors of these concentration camps reparation because they concluded that their detainment was done out of "race prejudice, war hysteria, and a failure of political leadership" and it had no military or security justification. The CWRIC's findings would have labeled President Roosevelt's actions as terrorism had they been perpetrated by anyone of Arab descent. Though the label was not implemented, our actions qualify as acts of terrorism according to its definition.

Very few Americans view the atomic bombs dropped on Hiroshima and Nagasaki as acts of terrorism, even though an overwhelming majority of the causalities were civilians. At the beginning of the Iraq War, the sentiment "nuke 'em all" was widespread. And the justification for the bombing of these cities in Japan, as well as Iraq, might sound eerily similar to the justification used by Muslims who use terrorism as a means to accomplish their goals. But the America of today should not be characterized by the mistakes of those of the past. Neither should Islam be demonized for what some Muslims have done. The Muslim must take the cue from America and The CWRIC and renounce the wrongs done in the name of Islam.

This comparison is not to vilify America or lighten the burden on terrorists, but to illustrate that there is a double standard here. Though later found to be completely erroneous, FDR sincerely believed that his actions were necessary. President Truman felt the use of the atomic bomb was absolutely necessary. The Palestinian, with every fiber of his being, believes that suicide bombing is the only means which he is afforded. Each of these persons knowingly harmed or killed innocent people through terrorism, yet only one party's belief in the necessity for their use of terrorism is not heard, accepted or even acknowledged. I am totally and completely against killing any innocent person, but we must realize that any person who is willing to do such a thing is in a state of desperation. We must ask, "Is the desperation warranted?" WHY are suicide bombings happening?

If you were living in a home and the police took over your home and gave it to me. What would you do? Suppose I gave you and your family the basement to live in, but you can't come out of the basement without being searched? So you decide to regain your home, but to your dismay the police are alongside me in keeping you in the basement. We take hold of your weapons, so as to discourage you from contemplating any uprising, and you must face your family daily. They live in the worse conditions. They have diseases with no medicine, they relieve themselves in the same place that they eat, they and you are illiterate. You feel if your home was taken by force, then it should be retrieved by force. In desperation, you fight with rocks, but I use a shotgun and I shot you down. My every action is sanctioned by the police and by my God. WHAT WOULD YOU DO? WHAT WOULD YOU DO?

It has long been the Muslim's claim that Palestine was unjustifiably taken from the Palestinians. Those who are pro- Israel say that Palestine was not a state because it did not have a name at the time. Is my house, not a house, if I don't have an address number? The Palestinian Muslims, Jews and Christians were all living on this land, when it was made legal for every Jew on earth to come and live in Palestine. The Jews of Germany were not the only Jews given shelter in Palestine, but all Jews from everywhere. Should not GERMANY be a better place where the Jews should be arbitrarily given land, since this is the place that the Holocaust victims were uprooted? Would it be permissible for the Native Americans to decide to reclaim their land from Americans and place us in concentration camps? Simply because you use to own a certain land does not automatically give you a right to indict the current residents, especially when the current residents were not the people who uprooted you. I never took anything from a Native American. They were displaced hundreds of years ago, whereas the Jews were displaced THOUSANDS of years ago. Like the Native Americans, the Palestinians were put in concentration camps, but Palestinians never discontinued the fight to reclaim their property. Therefore the inhabitants of their land are occupying it, while the war is still being waged.

The talk show host, Bill Maher (formerly of "Politically Incorrect" and now on "Real Time with Bill Maher") often criticizes the Bible and more specifically the Old Testament, for its violence and immorality, despite the fact that he is someone who supports the existence of Israel. Israel is a state which was brought into existence and maintains its existence, in Biblical times and today, through violence and immorality. How he cannot see the irony of denouncing the Old Testament and announcing his support for Israel is beyond understanding.

HOW MODERN ISRAEL WAS ESTABLISHED

In World War I, the British enlisted the help of Arabs in order to defeat the Ottoman Empire, which was in allegiance with Germany and in control of Palestine, at that time. For their assistance, Britain promised the Arabs control of all of the Arabs lands. But Britain also received help from their Jewish allies.

Perhaps the one man most responsible for the existence of Israel today is Dr. Chaim Weizmann. He was a scientist, the leader of the Zionists (those who seek to re-establish Israel as a state) for 30 years and the first

President of the State of Israel. At the age of 30, he moved to Great Britain. There he presented the British government with an invention in which he used corn to produce acetone, a solvent used in making explosives. The British used his new invention to defeat Germany in World War I. In exchange for Weizmann's help, Britain promised to fulfill the Zionist agenda and give the Jews a homeland. British Prime Minister Arthur Balfour initially wanted Uganda to be the Jewish homeland, but it was Weizmann who convinced Balfour to give Palestine to the Jews.

So Britain gave the Arabs some land and at the same time took Arabs land in Palestine and gave it to the Jews, disregarding the Palestinians who already lived there. We must remember that Jews were already living in Palestine and they, like the Palestinians, were living under Muslim rule by the Ottoman Empire. The Muslims and Jews were living in complete harmony under this Muslim rule, thus nullifying the accusation that Muslims and Jews are inherent enemies. If Balfour was without influence from Weizmann, there would be no Arab-Israeli conflict. Undoubtedly there would be a Ugandan-Israeli conflict. But the Promised Land, or Zion, described in the Jewish Torah is what the Zionists were looking for. Though many Israelis use the Jewish Torah to substantial their claim to the land, it is in fact a violation of the laws of the Jewish Torah to establish and maintain the land using military and financial aid from any other country. They are ordered not to borrow from any other country (Deut. 15:6), especially those countries which they deem as having any God beside the God of Israel, for example Christian nations which recognize Jesus as God.

KING DAVID HOTEL

Britain had power over the disputed land. When Jews began to pour in from all over the world, tensions began to build from the Palestinians, who were being replaced or displaced despite being the overwhelming majority. In 1880, there were about 24,000 Jews living in Palestine and about 376,000 Arabs. By 1914 both groups had grown rapidly, 615,000 Arabs and 85,000 Jews, yet it was the Jews who were given power over the Palestinians. Not only were the Holocaust survivors of WWII allowed to live in Palestine, but any Jew on earth was and is to this day given the opportunity to live in the land (America should be able to appreciate the problems that unlimited immigration can cause to the Palestinian Arab, due to its current problem with illegal immigration). After empowering the Jews at the Palestinians expense, the British government realized their error. As they came to understand that the introduction of Jews from all over the world would cause great conflict and push out the Palestinians, Britain began to try to change courses. Jews were entering Israel according to terms that they and Britain had agreed upon as legal immigration, but many Jews entered Palestine illegally. This caused Britain to place limitations on the Jewish immigration into Palestine. As a result Israeli terror groups assembled to attack British soldiers, civilians, and symbols in the land.

On July 22, 1946, a Zionist terror group called Irgun set off a bomb in The King David Hotel killing 91 people including 41 Arabs, 28 Britishers and 17 Jews. This was retaliation for Britain's investigation of the Jewish Agency and the arrests of over 2,500 Jews throughout Palestine for wrongdoing. Many historians mark this event as the beginning of modern day terrorism. The irony is that the hotel bombing was done with the explosives invented by Weizmann. Members of the terror group posed as Arabs delivering milk to gain access to their target without being detected. This plan was organized and arranged by Irgun leader, Menachem Begin, who has been called "the most successful terrorist leader of modern times." After this attack, Britain began to arrest and execute members of Irgun for their part in the bombings. Begin's group broke into Acre prison, kidnapped and hanged two British sergeants, Clifford Martin and Marvyn Paice, to convince the British to discontinue the death penalty on Irgun members.

"Growing numbers of British forces were deployed to quell the Jewish uprising, yet Begin managed to elude captivity, at times disguised as a rabbi. The British Security Service MI5 placed a 'dead-or-alive' bounty of £10,000 on his head after Irgun threatened 'a campaign of terror against British officials,' saying they would kill Sir John Shaw, Britain's Chief Secretary in Palestine. An MI5 agent codenamed Snuffbox also warned that Irgun had sleeper cells in London trying to kill members of British Prime Minister Clement Attlee's Cabinet." -Agent Snuffbox and an Israeli threat to kill Cabinet," Mail on Sunday (London), 5 March 2006, p.40.

Perhaps the reason that Irgun wished to kill members of Attlee's cabinet was because of this harsh but accurate account of the King David Hotel Bombing that Attlee gave to the House of Commons:

"Hon. Members will have learned with horror of the brutal and murderous crime committed yesterday in Jerusalem. Of all the outrages which have occurred in Palestine, and they have been many and horrible in the last few months, this is the worst. By this insane act of terrorism 93 innocent people have been killed or are missing in the ruins. The latest figures of casualties are 41 dead, 52 missing and 53 injured. I have no further information at present beyond what is contained in the following official report received from Jerusalem:

"It appears that after exploding a small bomb in the street, presumably as a diversionary measure -- this did virtually no damage -- a lorry drove up to the tradesmen's entrance of the King David Hotel and the occupants, after holding up the staff at pistol point, entered the kitchen premises carrying a number of milk cans. At some stage of the proceedings, they shot and seriously wounded a British soldier who attempted to interfere with them. All available information so far is to the effect that they were Jews. Somewhere in the basement of the hotel they planted bombs which went off shortly afterwards. They appear to have made good their escape."

Every effort is being made to identify and arrest the perpetrators of this outrage. The work of rescue in the debris, which was immediately organized, still continues. The next-of-kin of casualties are being notified by telegram as soon as accurate information is available. The House will wish to express their profound sympathy with the relatives of the killed and with those injured in this dastardly outrage." (House of Commons Debates, Hansard 425:1877-78 (23 July, 1946).

THE DEIR YASSIN MASSACRE

Another terror attack perpetrated by Irgun in collusion with another terror group called the Stern Gang was the Deir Yassin massacre on April 9, 1948. In order to build an airfield for Israel, Irgun went on the offensive and decided to take the land and kill or displace the 750 inhabitants of a small village called Deir Yassin. The death toll of this small village was staggering. Of the 750 Palestinians, at least 16% of the population was killed. The rested survived because they fled or were captured and sent to other Arab occupied lands. Many of the details of the massacre are best guesses. There had been reports of mass graves and many other atrocities. Of course, these accusations were called wild exaggerations by the Jewish government. They were afforded the opportunity to deny most claims because their soldiers set the dead on fire, destroying all the evidence.

This massacre resulted in the 1948 Palestinian Exodus. It was an Exodus from terrorism, which Zionists has called abandonment of their land, thus justifying its occupation. Menachem Begin, himself, admitted that the terror used in Deir Yassin was the reason for Palestinians' mass departure. And these Palestinians were not only Muslims, but Christians as well. Thousands of Christians were killed, thousands of Christians had their property confiscated and thousands of Christians were made refugees. Over 700,000 Palestinians packed up and left to secure their families safety from terrorism. Today there are an estimated 5,000,000 Palestinian refugees. As Shabir Ally, noted Muslim lecturer, suggested, if Israel wants to uphold true democracy, it would allow these five million people into their country to cast their votes on the future of the land. This is not a matter of religion. It is a matter of human rights. It should not take injustices done to your particular group for you to recognize and acknowledge the injustices done to another group.

If we look closely, it is crystal clear that these terror groups were government sponsored. They carried out the government of Israel's agendas. Irgun bombed buses, marketplaces and even hotels. They kidnapped and killed people to help build Israel and they effectively removed the supervision of Britain, the country that gave them Israel. Britain left the troubled country and Israel took complete control of the land. The Israeli government publicly denounced these terror groups' actions, but privately endorsed them. To illustrate that the public denunciation of the acts of terrorism were insincere, let's consider the appointed officials of Israel.

Begin, the leader of the terrorist group, Irgun, was elected Prime Minister of Israel in 1977. And in 1978, he was awarded a Nobel Peace Prize for his "efforts" to bring to peace to a land in which he perpetuated TERROR. The first President of Israel was Dr. Chaim Weizmann. His nephew and former member of Irgun Ezer Weizmann also became President of Israel. Benjamin Netanyahu, 2 time Prime Minister of Israel, even commemorated the 60 year anniversary of the King David Hotel Bombing in July 2006 to the chagrin of many Britons. Yitzhak Shamir, a leader of the Stern Gang, was infamous for his success in assassinations. He was responsible for the assassination of Lord Moyne, the British Resident Minister for the Middle East and his driver in November of 1944, as well as the assassination in 1948 of Count Folke Bernadotte, a United Nations Security Council mediator in the Arab-Israeli conflict. Yet Shamir became Israel's Foreign Minister and Prime Minister. It is very hypocritical for the state of Israel to denounce terrorism when it is founded on terrorism and its elected officials were those who orchestrated terrorist attacks on the non-Jews of Palestine.

The Israeli government in 1978 issued stamps commemorating Avraham Stern, from whom the terrorist Stern Gang was christened. Not only was Stern the leader of this terrorist organization, but he unsuccessful tried to negotiate with THE HITLER AND THE MUSSOLINI REGIME to establish Israel.

"BUT IT IS OUR COUNTRY!!!"

A correspondent of the German newspaper "The Frankfurter Zeitung," by the name of Leopold Weiss recalled a meeting that he had with the founder of Israel, Dr. Chaim Weizmann, at a friend's house in Jerusalem in 1922. Weiss, an Austrian German Jew "dared to question the unquestionable right of the Jews to the land of their forefathers"

"He (Weizmann) was talking of the financial difficulties which were besetting the dream of a Jewish National Home, and the insufficient response to this dream among people abroad; and I had the disturbing impression that even he, like most of the other Zionists, was inclined to transfer the moral responsibility for all that was happening in Palestine to the 'outside world.' This impelled me to break through the deferential

hush with which all the other people present were listening to him, and to ask: "What about the Arabs?"

I must have committed a faux pas by thus bringing a jarring note into the conversation, for Dr. Weizmann turned his face slowly toward me, put down the cup he had been holding in his hand, and repeated my question: "What about the Arabs ...?"

"Well – how can you ever hope to make Palestine your homeland in the face of the vehement opposition of the Arabs who, after all, are in the majority of the country?" The Zionist leader shrugged his shoulders and answered drily: "We expect they won't be in a majority after a few years."

"Perhaps so. You have been dealing with this problem for years and must know the situation better than I do. But quite apart from the political difficulties which Arab opposition may or may not put in your way – does not moral aspect of the question ever bother you? Don't you think that is wrong on your part to displace the people who have always lived in this country?"

"But it is our country," replied Dr. Weizmann, raising his eyebrows. "We are doing no more than taking back what we have wrongly been deprived of."

"But you have been away from Palestine for nearly two thousand years! Before that you had ruled this country, and hardly ever the whole of it, for less than five hundred years. Don't you think that the Arabs could, with equal justification, demand Spain for themselves – for, after all, they held sway in Spain for nearly seven hundred years and lost it entirely only five hundred years ago?"

Dr. Weizmann had visibly become impatient: "Nonsense. The Arabs had only conquered Spain; it had never been their original homeland, and so it was only right that in the end theywere driven out by the Spaniards."

"Forgive me," I retorted, "but it seems to me that there is some historical oversight here. After all, the Hebrews also came as conquerors to Palestine. Long before them were many other Semitic and non-Semitic tribes settled here – the Amorites, the Edomites, the Philistines, the Moabites, the Hitties. Those tribes continued living here even in the days of kingdoms of Israel and Judah. They continued living here after the Romans drove our ancestors away. They are living here today. The Arabs who settled in Syria and Palestine after their conquest in seventh century were always only a small minority of the population; the rest of what we describe today as Palestinians or Syrian "Arabs" are in reality only the Arabianized, original inhabitants of the country. Some of them became Muslims in the course of centuries, others remained Christians; the

Muslims naturally inter-married with their coreligionists from Arabia. But can you deny that the bulk of those people in Palestine, who speak Arabic, whether Muslims or Christians, are direct-line descendants of the original inhabitants; original in the sense of having lived in this country centuries before the Hebrews came to it?"
Dr. Weizmann smiled politely at my outburst and turned the conversation to other topics... "How is it possible, I wondered, for people endowed with so much creative intelligence as the Jews to think of the Zionist-Arab conflict in Jewish terms alone? Did they not realize that the problem of the Jews in Palestine could, in the long run, be solved only through co-operation with the Arabs? Were they so hopelessly blind to the painful future which their policy must bring?-to the struggles, the bitterness and the hatred to which the Jewish island, even if temporarily successful, would forever remain exposed in the midst of a hostile Arab sea?
And how strange, I thought, that a nation which had suffered so many wrongs in the course of its long and sorrowful diaspora was now, in single-minded pursuit of its own goal, ready to inflict a grievous wrong on another nation – and a nation, too, that was innocent of all that past Jewish suffering. Such a phenomenon, I knew, was not unknown to history; but it mademe, none the less, very sad to see it enacted before my eyes."
(The Road to Mecca, by Muhammad Asad pg 95-96)

Weiss wasn't necessarily trying to convince Weizmann to put an end to his plans to displace the Palestinians, but to at least give some consideration to the moral aspect and the repercussions of such an action. For this stance, Weiss was labeled and dismissed as an Arab sympathizer. But throughout his travels, he came to realize the truth of the religion of those whom he spoke up for. And in 1926, the Jewish Leopold Weiss became the Muslim Muhammad Asad.

OTHER QUOTES ABOUT THE ESTABLISHMENT OF ISRAEL

"Why should the Arabs make peace? If I was an Arab leader I would never make terms with Israel. That is natural: we have taken their country. Sure

God promised it to us, but what does that matter to them? Our God is not theirs. We come from Israel, but two thousand years ago, and what is that to them? There has been anti-Semitism, the Nazis, Hitler, Auschwitz, but was that their fault? They only see one thing: we have come here and stolen their country. Why should they accept that?"
-Quoted by Nahum Goldmann in Le Paraddoxe Juif (The Jewish Paradox),[This is the words of the first Prime Minister of Israel when the state was established, David Ben-Gurion. And these are the exact sentiments of the Palestinians and every Muslim in support of Palestine.]

"We must expel Arabs and take their places."
-David Ben Gurion, 1937, Ben Gurion and the Palestine Arabs, Oxford University Press, 1985.

"We must do everything to ensure they [the Palestinian refugees] never do return"
-David Ben-Gurion, in his diary, 18 July 1948, quoted in Michael Bar Zohar's Ben-Gurion: the Armed Prophet, Prentice- Hall, 1967, p. 157.

"We should prepare to go over to the offensive. Our aim is to smash Lebanon, Trans-Jordan, and Syria. The weak point is Lebanon, for the Moslem regime is artificial and easy for us to undermine. We shall establish a Christian state there, and then we will smash the Arab Legion, eliminate Trans-Jordan; Syria will fall to us. We then bomb and move on and take Port Said, Alexandria and Sinai."
-David Ben-Gurion, May 1948, to the General Staff. From Ben-Gurion, A Biography, by Michael Ben-Zohar, Delacorte, New York 1978.

The following are excerpts of suggestions made by Yisrael Koenig in the Koenig Memorandum:

On Population Control:

"Expand and deepen Jewish settlement in areas where the contiguity of the Arab population is prominent and where they number considerably more than the Jewish population: examine the possibility of diluting existing Arab population concentrations."

On Economic Control:

"We would act courageously and replace all the people who deal with the Arab sector on behalf of government institutions, the police and the parties, including policy-makers"

"The number if Arab employees should not exceed 20%"

"Reach a settlement with central marketing factors of various consumer goods that could neutralize and encumber Arab agents"

"The government must find a way to neutralize the payment of "big family" grants to the Arab population, either by linking them to the economic situation or by taking this responsibility from the national insurance system and transferring it to the Jewish Agency or to the Zionist Organization, SO THAT THE GRANT IS PAID TO JEWS ONLY. "

"Endeavor to have central institutions pay more attention in giving preferential treatment to Jewish groups or individuals rather than to Arabs."

On Education Control:

"The reception criteria for Arab university students should be the same as for Jewish students and this must also apply to the granting of scholarships. A meticulous implementation of these rules will produce a NATURAL SELECTION and will considerably reduce the number of Arab students." "Encourage the channeling of (Arab) students into technical professions, to physical and natural sciences. These studies leave less time for dabbling in nationalism and the dropout rate is higher."

"Make trips abroad for studies easier, while making the return and employment more difficult-this policy is apt to encourage their emigration."

On Law Enforcement:

"Introduce law suits and put into effect a number of court sentences, particularly in the sphere of INCOME TAX AND ILLEGAL BUILDING"

"Increase the presence of various police and security forces in the Arab streets to deter extremist circles and 'THOSE WHO ARE SITTING ON THE FENCE' and are likely to be dreawn into uprisings and demonstrations "

Koenig Memorandum or The Koenig Report is a confidential Israeli government document authored in 1976 by the Labor Party member, Yisrael Koenig. The document, which was accidentally leaked by an unknown source, reveals a multitude of strategies which have been used by the Israeli government to discriminate against non-Jews in Israel. Its main goal was to persuade non-Jews to leave Israel, which "ensures the long-term Jewish national interests."

Koenig expressed the need to "examine the possibility of diluting existing Arab population concentrations." The mindset embodied in this report is repulsive. It presupposes Jewish superiority over the Arabs, describing its academic achievements as "Natural Selection." To boast about a higher position gained by discrimination, deceit and criminal activity is asinine. This is documentation of racism and discrimination purposely done to another group of people. And this kind of agenda backed by the Israeli government is reminiscent of the American government's instituted laws to infringe upon the civil rights of its Black citizens. The Arabs of Palestine were already displaced from their homes, but this was not enough. They must be removed from the land of Israel completely. This kind of treatment of the Palestinians has caused them to have this same sentiment towards the Israelis, yet they are aggressively criticized for their feelings. The government of the state of Israel has been caught putting plans in motion to get rid of the Palestinians and no one bats an eye.

We constantly hear that the Palestinians are intent upon bring about the destruction of Israel. We are repeatedly told that they wish to wipe Israel off of the map. But I would like you to take a look at the map of the world and tell me, WHERE IS PALESTINE? It does not exist on a map. It has been divided into two territories, Gaza and the West Bank, which are under the authority of Israel. The citizens of Gaza and the West Bank cannot enter or leave freely and without Israeli military checkpoints. They cannot leave their shores. While we are being convinced that Palestinians wish for the eradication of Israel, Israel is effectively eradicating Palestine, into smaller and smaller territories throughout the years, using military occupation and illegal settlements. It is about time that we view the issue from both sides.

The hypocritical and one-sided view of the disputed land is the reason that people like Former President Jimmy Carter have begun to speak out against the injustices committed against the Palestinian people. Carter played a very pivotal role in promoting peace in that region during his presidency. He has been quoted as saying "The greatest commitment in my life has been trying to bring peace to Israel." In his book entitled "Palestine: Peace not Apartheid," Carter places much of the blame for the instability of the people on Israel. He has gotten waves of criticism for the stance that Israel is oppressing the Palestinians, as well as his usage of the word, "apartheid" in describing Palestine. To this criticism, Mr. Carter says "I feel completely at ease. I am not running for office. And I have Secret Service protection." Perhaps more qualified to apply the term of apartheid are Nelson Mandela and Bishop Desmond Tutu. Both men as fighters against South Africa's apartheid regime have declared Israel to be an apartheid state. Whether you agree or not with these views, it is about time that both parties get their time to speak. For too long it has been a monologue of Israelis and their supporters mounting their case for Israel, but progress will only occur with a dialogue, where the Palestinians are given equal opportunities. Then maybe we will come to a resolution.

As it pertains to religion, this book has shown that God promised the children of Israel, as Muslims or those who submit to the will of God, the land of Abraham (pbuh). It has also been established, from the Jewish Torah, that they have not fulfilled their end of the bargain. Therefore their agreement is void. In order for their promise to be renewed they must again follow the commandments of God, which are not in the Jewish Torah. The Qur'an is the last testament to mankind from God. In order to submit to God's will, you must first acknowledge his will. I believe this book solidifies my claim that the Jewish Torah is not the words of God, but the words of "those who write the book with their own hands and say this is from Allah, hoping to reap from it some small reward. Woe to them for what they do write and woe to them for what they earn" (Al-Qur'an 2:79). With this very short comparison of the Jewish Torah and the Qur'an in this book, I encourage you to find out for yourself if the Qur'an is indeed the words of God.

Some may say that all the difficulties that I have raised are due to problems in translations. This is why I specifically used a Jewish, instead of a Christian, source to quote from. If it is the case that volumes of books can be written about the mistakes of a certain book and all of them can be legitimately explained away due to poor translation, then it is time for a new translation. Believe me, if this is the case, I would be more than happy. My goal is not to bash the Jewish Torah or Judaism, but to give people the truth as I see it and if this book contributes in any way to the establishment of truth, then I have done what I intended to do. As Judaism and Islam closely resemble each other, any corrections to the misunderstandings of the Jewish Torah would most likely increase that resemblance.

ANTI-SEMITISM

The term, anti-Semitism, is most often defined as "hostility toward or discrimination against Jews as a religious group or race." This definition has made the religion of Judaism and its holy book, the Tanakh, almost completely immune to criticism. Because one is a Jew by race or religion, when someone criticizes a Jewish person, it is arbitrarily decided whether they are criticizing the race or the beliefs. Of course, judging someone on the basis of their race is unjustifiably wrong. But disagreeing with someone's beliefs is not wrong in any way. But no one wants to be labeled an anti-Semite. The term carries such a negative connotation that it is a deathblow to the character of anyone who is given this title, whether the allegations are true or false. Images of Germany, Nazis, Hitler and the Holocaust are drawn immediately when one speaks of anti-Semitism. Even the word, "Jew" seems as if it may offend. If an Arab man came on television and said, "the Jews should be the last to oppress others because they dealt with the harsh reality of oppression and slavery themselves," he might be wrongly called an anti-Semite for stated something which is actually true. We all know what "anti" means but what or who is a Semite.

The Semites are descendants from Shem, the son of Noah. The descendants of Shem include the Israelites, the Babylonians, the Assyrians, the Arameans and the ARABS. Is the aforementioned Arab man practicing self hatred or merely stating his point of view? I wonder how much anti-Semitism goes on when you see an Arab man on the street, at prayer, on an airplane or eating with his family. Perhaps such prejudice would be less prevalent if it was properly called anti-Semitism. What about the Jews around the world who speak out against the occupation of Palestine, are they anti-Semitic? We must be able to differentiate between criticism of a person simply because of his race and criticism of his belief system. I am not anti-Semitic. I am only anti-injustice. I am against injustices done by people of all races, religions and cultures to another.

It should be noted that most of the people known around the world as "Jews" are not Semites. That is to say that they are not descendants from Shem. 80% of all the Jews on earth are Ashkenazim Jews, meaning that they are Jews of the German rite. People like Albert Einstein, Sigmund Freud, and Karl Marx are Ashkenazi Jews. And because they are not Semitic, anti-Semitism is not the proper term to be applied to them in any case, whether it is race or religion. [It is puzzling that Judaism is not a faith which seeks converts when the major of its members are a product of conversion.] Even more important is the fact that Abraham (pbuh) and his offspring were descendants of Shem (Gen. 11:10-26) and it is Abraham's (pbuh) SEED which is to inherit the Promised Land. Yet most of the people in the land called Israel today are not of the seed of Abraham (pbuh). Most of the Jews of today are not the Hebrews of the Bible and they are not the children of Israel, but of German descent. In fact, the 2nd highest rate of skin cancer is found in the land of Israel because the climate is not conducive to their fair skin. The next highest rate of skin cancer is found in the Dutch of South Africa. An interesting parallel can be drawn here, because they too are not indigenous to the land and they face hardships due to the exposure to the sun. It could be said that both the Dutch and the Israelis put themselves in their respective predicament. And it should be noted that the Dutch are responsible for the Apartheid of South Africa, which became official government policy in May 1948, the same month and year that Israel declared itself a State.

I must emphasize that I do not believe Jews to be bad people. But many of them have been indoctrinated with the propaganda of the Jewish Torah. And those who have the belief that they are chosen by God and superior to others because of their race or ethnicity are the people that I am addressing. There are white and black religious groups, in America and perhaps all over the world, who seek to identify themselves as the chosen people spoken of in the Jewish Torah, in order to proclaim their superiority over everyone else and I have a problem with them also. It is the Jewish Torah which creates this kind of thinking. The point is that whoever the person and whatever their race, class or nationality, they are not superior to others based on this flimsy criteria. When I oppose Black Hebrew Israelites for claiming to be the Israelites of the Jewish Torah and claiming that blacks are superior to white people, I am not being anti-black, but anti-racism. I stand in opposition to racism by people of any color including my own.

It has been asserted that the Qur'an has an anti-Semitic undertone. Whether you believe the words of the Qur'an to be the words of God or the words of Muhammad (pbuh), it is crystal clear that the author asserts that the Children of Israel were chosen by God and they were blessed abundantly. The Qur'an's words against the children of Israel are in response to their rejection of God and his laws, which is duly noted throughout the Jewish Torah and the entire Hebrew scripture. The Jewish Torah on numerous occasions cited God's anger with the children of Israel, to such an extent that he regretted making man and he sought to wipe out the whole of humanity. Is the Jewish Torah, anti-Semitic? Is Moses (pbuh) anti-Semitic? Some of his last words are in total condemnation of the children of Israel.

Deuteronomy 31:27 For I know thy rebellion, and thy stiff neck: behold, while I am yet alive with you this day, ye have been rebellious against HaShem; and how much more after my death?
Deuteronomy 31:28 Assemble unto me all the elders of your tribes, and your officers, that I may speak these words in their ears, and call heaven and earth to witness against them.
Deuteronomy 31:29 For I know that after my death ye will in any wise deal corruptly, and turn aside from the way which I have commanded you; and evil will befall you in the end of days; because

ye will do that which is evil in the sight of HaShem, to provoke Him through the work of your hands.'

Moses (pbuh) loved the children of Israel. He did everything in his power to lead them to the straight path. This is a testament to his affinity for them. Anti-Semitism's definition includes the words "hostility" and "discrimination." You do not have genuine love for another person, if you are unjustifiably hostile to them or you discriminate against them. Moses (pbuh) wanted his brothers to have the same things he had. And so too, does every sincere Muslim on earth. The Jews believe in submission to God's will just as Muslims do. The real difference is that the Muslim believes that the Jews have the incorrect will. They have the will of man. They need the true will of God. The Qur'an calls for Muslims to give the greatest gift that they have to the Jews, their religion of truth, Islam. The fact that all Muslims want all Jews to be one with them as Muslims, not for political gain or material gain, but solely for the benefit of his Jewish brother, is the ultimate proof that the Muslim is not anti-Semitic, in any sense of the word.

FOR MORE INFORMATION READ

"Tanakh, The Holy Scriptures" by The Jewish Publication Society
"The Holy Qur'an" translated by Muhammad Pickthall or M.H.Shakir
"200 Ways the Qur'an Corrects the Bible" by Muhamed Ghounem
"Contradictions and Fallacies in the Bible" by K Alan
"The Road to Mecca" by Muhammad Asad
"Arabs and Israel: Conficlt or Conciliation" by Ahmed Deedat
"Judaism for Dummies" by Rabbi Ted Falcon, Ph.D. & David Blatner
"Zionism: The Real Enemy of the Jews" by Alan Hart
"Is the Bible God's Word?" By Ahmed Deedat
"What the Bible says about Muhammad" by Ahmed Deedat
"The Muslims at Prayer" by Ahmed Deedat

ABOUT THE AUTHOR

Mr. Campbell was raised attending both the Christian Church and the Muslim Mosque. He was always inquisitive about religion. Around the age of 14, he decided that Islam was the path for him. However, he was rather secretive about his belief due to the negative perception many had of the religion. When Islam became the topic of any discussion, he maintained the Islamic sympathizer role as the son of a Muslim, while being careful not to be identified as a Muslim himself. The stigma surrounding Islam and Muslims only intensified throughout the years, but so too did his desire to announce to the world that ISLAM IS THE TRUTH. Throughout his life, he had engage others in discussions on religion and a little over three years ago he realized that the issues that were raised in debate and in dialogue were issues which warranted extensive details, evidence and explanations. Drawing from all the books, lectures, and debates he come in contact with, and all the talks with Muslims, Christians, Jews, Hindus, atheists and agnostics, he set out to write one book which would convince all of the truth about the God of the universe. This one book blossomed into eight books which are written with the primary goal of proving the validity of Islam. It is with his sincerest effort that he wrote these books, with the hope that all readers will set aside their preconceived ideas and have an open mind.

BOOKS BY THIS AUTHOR INCLUDE:

"ISLAM IS THE TRUTH"
"JESUS WAS NOT CRUCIFIED"
"THE JEWISH TORAH IS NOT THE WORD OF GOD"
"THERE IS NO TRINITY"
"25 MYTHS ABOUT ISLAM"
"GOD THE IRRESISTIBLE"
"FAQs ABOUT ISLAM"
"WHAT GOD SAYS ABOUT JESUS"

FOR INFORMATION ON PURCHASING THESE BOOKS LOG ON TO WWW.ISLAMISTHETRUTH.ORG